Ways of Listening ∾

Ways of Listening

An Ecological Approach to the Perception
of Musical Meaning ～ ～ ～

ERIC F. CLARKE

OXFORD
UNIVERSITY PRESS

2005

OXFORD
UNIVERSITY PRESS

Oxford University Press, Inc., publishes works that further
Oxford University's objective of excellence
in research, scholarship, and education.

Oxford   New York
Auckland   Cape Town   Dar es Salaam   Hong Kong   Karachi
Kuala Lumpur   Madrid   Melbourne   Mexico City   Nairobi
New Delhi   Shanghai   Taipei   Toronto

With offices in
Argentina   Austria   Brazil   Chile   Czech Republic   France   Greece
Guatemala   Hungary   Italy   Japan   Poland   Portugal   Singapore
South Korea   Switzerland   Thailand   Turkey   Ukraine   Vietnam

Published by Oxford University Press, Inc.
198 Madison Avenue, New York, New York 10016

www.oup.com

Oxford is a registered trademark of Oxford University Press

Library of Congress Cataloging-in-Publication Data
Clarke, Eric F.
Ways of listening : an ecological approach to the perception of musical meaning /
Eric F. Clarke.
   p. cm.
Includes bibliographical references and index.
ISBN-13 978-0-19-515194-7
ISBN 0-19-515194-1
1. Musical perception. 2. Nature (Aesthetics). 3. Music—History and criticism.
I. Title.
ML3845 .C494 2005
781.1'7—dc22   2005003412

9 8 7 6 5 4 3 2 1

Printed in the United States of America
on acid-free paper

Acknowledgments ⁓

I am very fortunate to have had help of various kinds from numerous people while I was working on this book. Sometimes a small comment made a bigger difference than might have been suspected, and in other cases people were incredibly generous with their time and expertise. Many thanks to: John Churcher, Frances Clarke, John Clarke, Nicholas Cook, Alan Costall, Nicola Dibben, Cathy Ferreira, Marianne Fillenz, Charlie Ford, Carol Krumhansl, Hugh Nankivell, and Luke Windsor. I am grateful to Maribeth Anderson Payne, who while at OUP first showed interest in the proposal, and to Kim Robinson and Eve Bachrach, who helped to see it through to completion.

The completion of this book was made possible by a period of study leave from the University of Sheffield and a period of matched leave funded by the Arts and Humanities Research Board under their Research Leave Scheme.

Earlier versions of parts of this book appeared in two journal articles; the material is included here by permission of the publishers. The articles are "Meaning and the specification of motion in music" *Musicae Scientiae*, V (2001) 213–234; and "Subject-position and the specification of invariants in music by Frank Zappa and P. J. Harvey" *Music Analysis*, 18 (1999) 347–374 (Oxford: Blackwell Publishers). Words and music for "Taut" by Jean Harvey & John Parish, © 1996 Hot Head Music Ltd. and Rondor Music (London) Ltd. (50%). EMI Music Publishing Ltd., London WC2H 0QA. Reproduced by permission of IMP Ltd. All rights reserved.

Contents ∼

Ways of Listening ∼

Introduction

Imagine that you are tidying your desk and come across an unlabeled CD. Not knowing what it is (it could be a backup disk, some student work, a CD of sound examples) you put it into your CD player and press the play button. The first track starts with a kind of blustery, rustly, crackly sound—hard to recognize to begin with—and then clearly the sound of someone eating crisps. This must be some studio project belonging to a student, you think, and curious to discover what else is on it (now that you know that it is audio and not data!) you skip to the next track—which starts with African percussion sounds over a jazzy bass line and what sounds like a sampled mbira. This is definitely someone else's CD, so you press stop, eject the CD and wonder who it belongs to and how to get it back to its rightful owner.

This brief imagined example illustrates some of the themes concerning sound, music, perception, and meaning that run through this book. First, it illustrates how the primary function of auditory perception is to discover what sounds are the sound *of*, and what to do about them: these are the sounds of someone else's CD, and you need to find a way to get it back to that person. Second, it suggests that when you hear what sounds are the sounds of, you then have some understanding of what those sounds mean: the recorded sounds of someone eating crisps and of African-influenced world-beat music are in this case the sounds of someone else's CD. Third, it shows that sounds are often the sounds of all kinds of things at the same time: the first track of this imagined CD presents the sounds of crackly cellophane packaging (or is it blustery wind on the microphone?), and crisps being eaten (or is it celery? or the crunching of leaves?), and location recording, and student work; the second track is the sound of pop music, and of a sampled mbira (or is it a marimba?), and of the influence of jazz, and of a European idea of "the sound of Africa."

My imagined scenario also illustrates the way in which musical sounds take place in a wider context of other sounds. The tidying up that uncovered this mystery CD would have generated all kinds of rustling and shuffling sounds as papers and other objects were moved around, and perhaps a clatter or thump as something fell to the floor and you looked down to retrieve it: it is in this context that the sounds of the CD are heard. If, not knowing what was on the CD, you half expected the chaotic electronic noises that you get when you try to play a data CD, then the crackly sounds of cellophane packaging being opened at the start of the first track might be momentarily disorienting. Are they on the CD or caused by something in the room? Musical sounds inhabit the same world as other sounds, and while the majority of writing on music, and music perception, has tended to cordon off music from the rest of the acoustical environment, it is self evident that we listen to the sounds of music with the same perceptual systems that we use for all sound.[1]

Many previous approaches to musical meaning have adopted either a linguistic or a more generally semiotic perspective, rather than the perceptual approach that I adopt here. The subtitle of this book declares that it is an ecological approach to the perception of musical meaning. What do I mean by the perception of musical meaning, and what is an ecological approach? Perception is the awareness of, and continuous adaptation to, the environment, and, on the basis of that general definition, the perception of musical meaning is therefore the awareness of meaning in music while listening to it. It can be distinguished from musical meaning that arises out of thinking about music, or reflecting on music, when not directly auditorily engaged with music. Under those circumstances music is imagined or recalled, rather than perceived, since nothing is going on in the peripheral auditory system (the outer, middle and inner ear).[2] Ecology is the study of organisms in relation to their environment, and the approach to perception presented in this book is characterized as ecological because it takes as its central principle the relationship between a perceiver and its environment. While there is a biological thread running through the book—in terms of ecology and adaptation, and a concern with the organism and its environment—I do not attempt to describe or explain the structure or function of the auditory system. Other books already do that authoritatively (e.g. Handel, 1989; Moore, 1997). My main aim is to discuss the ways in which listeners interact with the general auditory, and more specifically musical, environment: to discuss listening to music as the continuous awareness of meaning, by considering musical materials in relation to perceptual capacities.

The totality of "music," in even just one culture or subculture, is a large and complex web of phenomena, but this book will deal almost exclusively with the sound component of music. This concentration on sound comes not from a belief that the "essence" of music is sound, but from a recognition that sound is a component of all musical cultures, and that despite extensive writing in music theory, aesthetics, and the psychology of music, there is still a fragmented and contradictory understanding of what listening to music "feels like," and of how that experience might be understood and explained.

Music and Ecological Theory

The aim of this book is to understand music in the light of the ecological perceptual theory proposed by James Gibson (e.g. 1966; 1979) and others (see Heft 2001). Perhaps because of his own progressive deafness, Gibson developed his ideas much less in relation to auditory perception than vision, and made only the most cursory reference to music. Since Gibson's death in 1979, however, others have explored the potential of an ecological approach, first in relation to auditory perception in general, and more recently in relation to music. Vanderveer's doctoral thesis (Vanderveer 1979) is an important starting point, as are studies by Warren and Verbrugge (1984) and Gaver (1993a; 1993b). Two influential books (Handel 1989; Bregman 1990) also applied certain aspects of the ecological approach to auditory perception, both of which featured some discussion of music. Bregman's *Auditory Scene Analysis* in particular has been regarded as a landmark in the study of auditory perception, though neither Handel nor Bregman adopt a wholly ecological outlook.[3]

In the last twenty years, however, there have been various attempts to apply ecological perceptual theory to music in different ways.[4] The most comprehensive body of work in this respect has been that of Windsor, who in a series of publications (Windsor 1994; 1995; 1996a; 1996b; 1997; 2000; 2004) has discussed a whole variety of attributes of acousmatic music (that is, music presented over loudspeakers or headphones) from an ecological perspective, as well as more generally considering the relationship between ecology and semiotics. Finally, although not explicitly within an ecological framework, two electroacoustic composers, Dennis Smalley (1986; 1992; 1997) and John Young (1996), have written a number of important articles which discuss acousmatic music from a perspective that has significant commonalities with the approach developed by Windsor and with the ecological approach as a whole.

Listening and Meaning

In ecological theory, perception and meaning are closely related. When people perceive what is happening around them, they are trying to understand, and adapt to, what is going on. In this sense they are engaged with the meanings of the events in their environment. As I explore further in the next chapter, to hear a sound and recognize what it is (for example the sound of the mail being delivered through the letterbox) is to understand its perceptual meaning, which will result in corresponding actions. By contrast, to hear a sound and *not* recognize what it is, is to fail to understand its meanings and thus to act appropriately. For example, if I hear a regular sound from my back wheel as I cycle along and don't recognize that it is made by a bulge in the tyre rubbing against the frame, then I will fail to understand what it means and that I need to stop and do something about it. Similarly, if at a concert I hear some sounds that I identify as leading up to the final cadence of a tonal piece of music, I understand an aspect of their meaning (final closure) and can prepare myself for the applause that will follow. By contrast, if I hear some sounds and fail to recognize them as pre-performance tuning, I will fail to understand that the "music proper" has not yet begun.

This view of meaning, closely tied to perception and action, is somewhat different from the many views of musical meaning that have been proposed within the frameworks of philosophical aesthetics (e.g. Kivy 1990; Davies 1994; Scruton 1997), phenomenology (e.g. Clifton 1983), semiotics (e.g. Nattiez 1990; Agawu 1991; Monelle 1992, 2000; Hatten 1994; Tarasti 1994), hermeneutics (e.g. Kramer 2001; 2003), multimedia (e.g. Cook 1998a; 2002), and social theory (e.g. Green 1988; Small 1998; DeNora 2000). Although all these authors give some consideration to the experience of hearing musical sounds, none of them is primarily concerned with explaining how that experience comes about. Most writers on the subject assume that sounds are picked up in one way or another, form basic units of some kind (notes, motifs, melodies, textures, etc.), and are organized into structures, but that the perceptual processes involved play little or no role in a theory of musical meaning. The explanation of meaning is to be found elsewhere—in theories of expression, semiotics, or social construction, for instance. By contrast, listening occupies a central position throughout this book, based on the proposition that the experience of musical meaning is fundamentally—though not exclusively—a perceptual experience. There is of course meaning in remembered and imagined music, and even in music that a person has read or heard *about* but never actually *heard*, but since none of these experiences involve any active engagement with the auditory environment, this is not perceptual meaning.

Psychology and Musicology

My approach addresses the perception of musical meaning from psychological and broadly musicological perspectives. On the one hand I argue the case for the explanatory power of certain general perceptual principles that apply to all human beings; and on the other hand I look at the particular consequences of those principles in contexts that are historically and culturally specific. As the outline of the book makes clear (discussed below), some chapters offer explanations, while others raise questions and explore consequences.

Since the 1980s, a partial convergence between the psychology of music and musicology has taken place (see also Clarke 2003 for a discussion). Some musicologists have adopted perceptual principles in their consideration of musical material and listeners' engagement with that material (e.g. Lerdahl and Jackendoff 1983; Cook 1990; Nattiez 1990; Cumming 2000; or, at an earlier stage, Meyer 1956), and some psychologists have not only accepted music as a legitimate domain in which to do research but have also tried to integrate the cultural and historical condition of musical materials into psychological research (e.g. Krumhansl 1995; 1998). Nonetheless, psychology and musicology have rather different basic agendas: psychology as a (social) science is fundamentally concerned with general principles of human behavior and mental life, understood from a contemporary perspective, and with an eye to "timeless laws," while musicology is more closely focused on particular manifestations, understood in their historical and cultural specificity, and with a strong sense of the provisional and shifting nature of that understanding. Since these differences have sometimes led to a degree of mutual frustration or incomprehension, I hope to show that the two disciplines can be combined in a fruitful and stimulating manner.

History, Repertory, and Cultures

My primary focus is contemporary listening—the experiences of listeners at the start of the twenty-first century. But those listening attitudes and practices did not just appear from nowhere: they have their own history and have come about by means of a historical process that continues to exert its influence. Understanding the perception of musical meaning therefore involves a historical dimension that surfaces in different ways, and to differing extents, in the chapters that follow. In a similarly heterogeneous way, I deal with a mixture of Western art music, and pop music, in order to show that the ideas apply equally well (though perhaps in different ways) to a variety of musical styles and traditions—to score-based and studio-based music, to instruments and to voices, to "absolute" music and to music with texts, to "art" music and to pop. The repertory does not extend beyond a subset of Western traditions, however, since that is where my experience and expertise lie. Nonetheless there is evidence that the ideas discussed here apply in interesting ways to other musical traditions (see Baily 1996). Indeed many aspects of ethnomusicological theory, with its attention to the relationships between musical practices and their cultural and natural environments, and the close relationship between perception, knowledge, and action in the study of musical cultures, are not only consistent with an ecological view but in some cases engage with it quite explicitly (e.g. Clayton 2001; Feld 1994).

The overall plan of the book moves from a predominantly scientific to a predominantly cultural perspective. Chapter 1 presents the theoretical principles on which most of the rest of the book is based—James Gibson's ecological approach to perception and developments of that theory in relation to sound and music. An important part of this discussion is a consideration of the relationship between nature and culture in perception, and specifically of the perception of "everyday" and "musical" sounds. Chapter 2 is an illustration of the way in which the theory proposed in chapter 1 might apply to a rather more extended musical example than the "sound clips" that have been featured so far: Jimi Hendrix's performance of "The Star Spangled Banner" recorded at Woodstock in 1969. In my analysis I attempt to show how different attributes of the perceived meaning of this music—relating to sound, structure, and ideology—coexist and are simultaneously available.

Chapters 3 and 4 address different aspects of the experience of subjectivity in music. Chapter 3 looks at the way in which motion and agency are perceived in music, and the consequences of this for a listener's sense of subjective engagement with musical materials. Chapter 4 examines the ways in which music influences or determines a particular listening attitude, or "subject-position," in relation to its material. Part of a listener's experience of music is the manner in which he or she is invited to engage with the "subject matter" of the music—seriously, ironically, authentically, in an alienated manner, with disbelief or humor. An analysis of two pop songs shows how this can be understood when the subject matter is substantially defined by textual content, and shorter analyses of instrumental music show how similar principles might apply in the absence of text.

Much of the music discussed in the book up to this point is either closely associated with texts or drama or has a well-defined social function. Chapter 5 considers the so-called absolute and autonomous music of the Western art music tradition, and autonomous or structural listening, in the light of ecological perceptual theory. Despite the apparent incompatibility between ecology and autonomy, I argue that ecological theory can shed light on the perceptual meaning of music from this tradition too. Chapter 6 demonstrates this with a perceptual analysis of a piece that is firmly within this absolute and autonomous tradition: the first movement of Beethoven's String Quartet in A minor, Op. 132. Finally, the conclusion brings together the themes of the book and addresses once again the relationship between perception and action in music, and the opportunities, values, and functions that music presents to a listener.

Music Perception, Information Processing, and Ecological Psychology

Consider once again the sounds from the unlabeled CD with which this chapter began, and the various ways in which you might hear them: as someone eating crisps, or perhaps celery, or walking on dry leaves; as friable objects being broken and pulverised; as a collection of semi-regular noise bursts with a predominance of high frequencies and no clear sinusoidal components; and so on. Taken together, these various possible responses seem to suggest that the sounds of the world reach our ears in a very indeterminate raw state, and that individual perceivers then make sense of them according to a whole range of factors: the specific context of the sounds, what the listeners were hearing most recently, differences in how they focus on the sounds, their previous experience or training, and so on—in short a whole variety of "processing" differences largely based on mental representations or memory processes of one sort or another. This is, broadly speaking, what might be called an "information-processing" approach to perception, and, from the 1970s until recently, it has been the dominant approach in music perception, as well as auditory perception and perceptual psychology more generally. My purpose here is to give a brief account of the information-processing approach, to point out some of its theoretical limitations, and then to consider the alternative offered by ecological theory.

A general outline of the information-processing view is as follows. In William James's famous phrase, the environment is regarded as a "blooming buzzing confusion" (James 1892: 16)—as a maelstrom of sensory stimulation which perceiving organisms organize and interpret with the processes and structures of their perceptual and cognitive apparatus. In other words, structure is not in the environment: it is imposed on an unordered or highly complex world by perceivers. This is a simplified and rather polarized version of the information-processing outlook, but in a variety of ways it has had a profound impact on the way in which the perception of music has been approached. Perhaps the most obvious influence is the almost ubiquitous conception of music perception as a set of stages or levels, proceeding from simpler and more stimulus-bound properties through to more complex and abstract characteristics that are less closely tied to the stimulus and are more the expression of general cognitive schemata and cultural conventions. Figure I.1 schematically represents this progression.

The ubiquity of this view can be seen in the way in which studies of music perception nearly always proceed from psychoacoustics (studies of the relationship between the physical properties of stimuli and their perceptual counterparts) to more cognitive studies (the organization of these primary psychoacoustical properties into more elaborated structures such as motifs and rhythmic groups), and finally to the abstract structures of larger stretches of music. In a book widely regarded as a primary reference volume on the psychology of music, the editor of the volume states:

> In this chapter we shall examine ways in which pitch combinations are abstracted by the perceptual system. First we shall enquire into the types of abstraction that give rise to the perception of local features, such as intervals, chords, and pitch classes. . . . Other low-level abstractions result in

Domain	Discipline

Mental/Social/Cultural   **Aesthetics/Sociology/Critical Theory**

Aesthetic value
Reference
Meaning

Mental   **Cognition**

Form
Tonality
Scale systems
Melodic organization
Meter
Etc.

Physical/Mental   **Psychoacoustics**

Basic attributes of sounds:
Pitch
Timbre
Rhythmic categories
Auditory streaming
Etc.

Physical   **Acoustics**

Sounds in the environment

Figure I.1   A schematic representation of the basic outlines of an
information-processing approach to music perception.

the perception of global features, such as contour. Next we
shall consider how combinations of features are abstracted
so as to give rise to perceptual equivalences and similarities. We shall then examine how these higher-level abstrac-
tions are themselves combined according to various rules.
(Deutsch 1999: 349)

The top of this pyramid of processing (which is arguably the goal of the whole sequence of processes), though often rather poorly defined or described, can be conceived as conscious or unconscious experiences of some kind which may or may not be expressible as named events or actions ("someone playing slide guitar," "the opening of the Rite of Spring," "a nursery rhyme in G major").

Information-processing accounts recognize that the flow of information is not unidirectional: as higher level interpretations emerge, they influence the processing of new information (a mechanism known as top-down, or concept-driven, processing) just as new information has the capacity to overturn or modify an emerging interpretation with which it conflicts (bottom-up, or data-driven, processing). Indeed top-down processing starts before the interpretation of any specific events has even got under way, since perception is always influenced and informed by whatever was happening immediately beforehand, as well as by more generalized preconceptions and expectations derived from previous experience. The variables of top-down processing therefore provide a clear and straightforward way in which to account for particular individuals' differing interpretations: differences in mind-set when a stimulus is encountered can feed down through a number of levels of processing and cause individuals to arrive at different outcomes. Equally, if the stimulus material itself is weakly or ambiguously structured, even a small difference of emphasis at some stage in processing might be enough for distinct processing paths to be followed from there on up through the system. Differences of this kind are offered as explanations for the multiple interpretations of visual and auditory illusions, or of poorly structured but suggestive arrays such as the Rorschach "inkblot" test, or acoustic collages (in which listeners may be quite convinced that they can hear all kinds of things that are not there).

The information-processing approach has a number of positive attributes: it offers a clearly structured route from simple to complex properties; it is consistent with the hierarchy of processing stages used in many computational approaches (feature extraction of one kind or another, or hierarchical pattern matching) but nonetheless avoids being too deterministic, by virtue of the interaction of top-down and bottom-up processing; and it reflects an assumption, or belief, that listeners are more immediately aware of the simple features of musical sounds than they are of higher-level characteristics, which are regarded as more abstract, complex, and remote.

However there are some significant problems with it. First, it relies very heavily on the idea of mental representations, both as the final state that the system achieves, and as intermediate stages along the way. The nature and existence of these representations is purely conjectural (they are inferred in order to account for behavior), and more fundamentally they suffer from the "homunculus" problem: a representation only has value or purpose if there is someone or something to perceive or use it, which leads to an infinite regress of homunculi inside the perceiver's mind, each of which "reads" and in turn generates an internal representation. Rather than making use of the structure that is already out there in the environment, the outside world is needlessly and endlessly internalized and duplicated (literally "re-presented"). Second, the standard information-processing account tends to be disembodied and abstract, as if perception was a kind of reasoning or problem-solving process, reflecting the strong influence of cybernetics, information theory, and artificial intelligence on cognitive psychology. Perception is treated as a kind of disinterested contemplation, with no connection to action—which bears little relationship to the essentially exploratory and orienting function of perception in the life of an organism. And finally, perception is characterized as working primarily from the bottom up (despite the incorporation of "top-down" processes), with more complex levels constructed from the outputs of lower-level, more primitive processes. Direct experience suggests that this is wrong: if you hear a burst of music from someone's radio, for instance, it is more likely that you will be able to say what style of music it is (opera, hip-hop, Country and Western) than to identify specific pitch intervals, or its key, meter, and instrumentation. In other words, people seem to be aware of supposedly "high-level" features much more directly and immediately than the lower-level features that a standard information-processing account suggests they need to process first.

More extensive considerations of the relationship between ecological psychology and the dominant cognitivism of contemporary psychology have been presented by Neisser (1976), who attempts an accommodation between the two, and in the collection edited by Still and Costall (1991), which depicts the relationship in more oppositional terms. My purpose here has been to do no more than present the basic orientation of the dominant paradigm in music perception research, and to point out some of its shortcomings. The next chapter argues for an alternative to this general outlook, based on the ecological perceptual theory of James Gibson and those who have taken up and developed his ideas.

I ⌇

Perception, Ecology, and Music

The Ecological Approach to Perception

Rather than considering perception to be a constructive process, in which the perceiver builds structure into an internal model of the world, the ecological approach emphasizes the structure of the environment itself and regards perception as the pick-up of that already structured perceptual information. The simple, but far-reaching, assertion is that the world is *not* a "blooming buzzing confusion", but is a highly structured environment subject to both the forces of nature (gravity, illumination, organic growth, the action of wind and water) and the profound impact of human beings and their cultures; and that in a reciprocal fashion perceivers are highly structured organisms that are adapted to that environment.

> The environment described [here] is that defined by ecology. Ecology is a blend of physics, geology, biology, archeology, and anthropology, but with an attempt at unification. The unifying principle has been the question of what can stimulate a sentient organism. (Gibson 1966: 29)

What is important is to consider what is *directly specified* by environmental information—not what a perceiving organism can interpret in, or construct from, a stimulus. The shape, mass, reflectance, density, and texture of a physical object directly determine the stimulus information that it gives off in different sensory domains when it is illuminated, struck, heated, scraped, blown with a stream of air, etc. For example, a hollow piece of wood will differentially reflect light of certain wavelengths according to its composition and the manner in which it has been cut and treated, and will vibrate with a certain pattern of frequencies if struck by another object (and as a function of the hardness and mass of that object) according to the degree to which it has been hollowed, and the specific size and shape of the cavity. This information directly specifies properties of the object itself to an organism equipped with an appropriate perceptual system. The amplitude and frequency distribution of the sounds emitted when this piece of hollowed wood is struck are a direct consequence of the physical properties of the wood itself—are an "imprint" of its physical structure—and an organism does not have to do complex processing to "decode" the information within the source: it needs to have a perceptual system that will *resonate* to the information:

> Instead of supposing that the brain constructs or computes the objective information from a kaleidoscopic inflow of sensations, we may suppose that the orienting of the organs of perception is governed by the brain so that the whole system of input and output resonates to the external information. (Gibson 1966: 5)

This "resonance" or "tuning" of the perceptual system to environmental information is different from the resonance of a string or hollow tube, for example, since these are fixed, and will only resonate to a specific kind of event—a particular frequency. The C-string of a cello, for example, will resonate sympathetically to a C sounded by another nearby instrument (or to some of the subharmonics of that C) but will not resonate to other kinds of sounds. Nor is this tuning like an analogue radio receiver, which can be tuned to any one of a great variety of broadcast frequencies but which needs someone to turn the knob. Perception is a *self*-tuning process, in which the pick-up of environmental information is intrinsically reinforcing, so that the system self-adjusts so as to optimize its resonance with the environment: "A system 'hunts' until it achieves clarity," wrote Gibson (1966: 271), a little like the scanning of a modern digital tuner, a device Gibson never encountered.

If ecological theory was simply the claim that organisms resonate to environmental information, which in turn directly specifies the objects and events from which it emanates, it would have little explanatory value: perception would be no more than a magical affinity between a perfectly structured environment and a miraculously endowed and adapted perceiver. There are three factors, however, that make the theory both more realistic and more interesting: the relationship between perception and action; adaptation; and perceptual learning.

Perception and Action

When humans and other animals perceive the world, they do so actively. Perception is essentially exploratory, seeking out sources of stimulation in order to discover more about the environment. This operates in so many ways and so continuously that it is easy to overlook: we detect a sound and turn to it; we catch sight of an object, turn our eyes to it, lean forward and reach out to touch it; we get a whiff of something and deliberately breathe in through the nose to get a better sense of its smell. These and countless other examples illustrate the constant orienting of the organism to its environment, the constant search to optimize and explore the source of stimulation. Actions lead to, enhance, and direct perception, and are in turn the result of, and response to, perception. Resonance is not passive: it is a perceiving organism's active, exploratory engagement with its environment.

In the circumstances of entertainment and aesthetic engagement, however, overt manifestations of the perception-action cycle are often blocked or transformed, as Windsor (1995; 2000) has also discussed. Watching films and television, looking at paintings or sculpture in a gallery, and listening to music in a concert hall deliberately place perceivers in a relationship with the objects of perception that prevents them from acting upon or exploring those objects in an unhindered fashion. Many of the reactions that people have to these special circumstances (reaching out to touch a sculpture; approaching or standing back from a painting; laughing, crying, or flinching at a film; foot- and finger-tapping in response to music) are a residue of the more usual relationship between perception and action, as are the specific conventions that regulate these reactions (ritualized audience participation at pantomimes, "Please do not touch" signs at exhibitions, darkened auditoria, socially enforced silence and immobility at concerts, applause at regulated moments). The interruption or suspension of the perception-action cycle that characterizes some forms of aesthetic engagement is, of course, culturally specific; it is at its most extreme in some of the "high" art forms of the West and in circumstances in which formal ceremony and aesthetics interact. In many other contexts (folk traditions, popular cultures, some experimental art and music), active participation is the norm. The specific consequences of what might be called the contemplative or "disinterested" (Meidner 1985) perceptual attitude required or encouraged by the autonomous art forms of the West is an issue I take up again in chapter 5.

Adaptation

Organisms and their environments are constantly changing. The "goodness of fit" between an organism and its environment is not a matter of chance: it is the product of mutual adaptation brought about by an evolutionary process. The giraffe's long neck in an environment of savannah dotted with thorny trees is not a lucky break: it is the result of an adaptation that has left the giraffe as a successful competitor in an environment where the ability to reach the high branches of trees with sharp thorns lower down is an advantage. Similarly, the fact that the human basilar membrane demonstrates a logarithmic frequency distribution over much of its length (i.e., a fixed distance on the basilar membrane corresponds to a roughly constant ratio of frequencies) is no miracle of divine design or happy accident: it confers an advantage in a world where struck and blown objects tend to radiate sounds with harmonic series properties; and it is a particular advantage in a species for which speech and other forms of vocal/auditory communication are so important. It allows, for instance, for the equivalence of the same pitch profile in different registers—an important attribute when trying to respond appropriately to the vocalizations of individuals with different vocal ranges (men and women, adults and juveniles).

The resonance of a perceptual system with its environment is a product of evolution and adaptation in the same way that an organism's feeding behavior is adapted to the available food supply. It is no miracle that rabbits "resonate" with grassland: not only are they adapted to compete extremely well in that physical environment, but their presence in such an environment directly contributes to the continuation and even expansion of that environment itself. By eating the shoots of tree and bush seedlings that might otherwise compete with the grass, the rabbits help to create and sustain the environment in which they thrive.

Without suggesting too simplistic a leap from rabbits and grassland to humans and music, the same interdependency and mutual adaptation nonetheless apply. Human beings have exploited natural opportunities for music making (the acoustical characteristics of materials and the action-possibilities of the human body) and have also adapted themselves to those opportunities, and enhanced those opportunities, through tool-making of one sort or another—from drilled bones, through catgut and wooden boxes to notational systems, voltage-controlled oscillators and iPods. Once made, all these artifacts help both to sustain existing musical behaviors (i.e., they help to perpetuate the musical ecosystem) and to make new behaviors possible. This mutual adaptation between human beings and their (musical) environment is neither reducible to conventional evolutionary principles, nor is it independent of them: culture and biology are tangled together in complex ways, but nonetheless constitute a single connected system (see Cross 2003).

Perceptual Learning

Adaptation between an organism and its environment occurs over evolutionary time, not in the life span of a single individual. But this does not mean that individuals come into the world with perceptual characteristics that remain fixed and determined throughout their lives: from the moment of their first encounters with the world, organisms are immersed in a continual process of perceptual learning—a matter to which the ecological approach to perception has paid considerable attention, in particular through the work of Eleanor Gibson (e.g. Gibson 1969). Cognitive psychology has also recognized the importance of changes in the perceptual capacities of humans and other animals, but has tended to treat the question in terms of the enrichment, or increased "coding power" of perception through experience and learning (as discussed in Gibson and Gibson 1955). According to a cognitive view, perceptual skills develop through the accumulation of knowledge that guides and informs them, and which fills in the information that is missing in a chaotic and imperfect environment. By contrast, the ecological approach views perceptual learning as progressive *differentiation*, perceivers becoming increasingly sensitive to distinctions within the stimulus information that were always there but previously undetected. A newborn human infant is equipped with a relatively small number of very powerful, but as yet rather undifferentiated, perceptual capacities. Exposure to the environment shapes these perceptual capacities, and distinctions that previously went unnoticed become detectable. As the infant explores these new discoveries, further distinctions that were previously unperceivable are revealed, and a cascade of successive differentiations ensues.

The overwhelming majority of this perceptual learning occurs "passively"—though this is a misleading term. What is meant is that there is no explicit *training* involved, no human supervisor pointing out distinctive features and appropriate responses. It is "passive" in the sense that it is not under the direct guidance of any external human agency, but it is, of course, profoundly active from the perspective of the organism itself. As already observed, perception and action are inextricably bound together, and the differentiation of attention that is described here takes place because the actions of the organism on the environment reveal previously unnoticed distinctions which in turn result in modified actions.

As a musical example of passive perceptual learning, consider a young child's discovery of loudness and pitch on a xylophone. On first encountering a xylophone, the child's more-or-less unregulated experiments with hands or sticks will result in all kinds of accidental sounds. With unsupervised investigation, the child may discover that different kinds of actions (with more force/with less force, to the left-hand side of the object/to the right-hand side of the object, with the fingers/with a stick) give rise to differentiated results (louder/softer, low pitched/high pitched, sharp attack/dull attack), and even that these distinctions can themselves be used to achieve other goals—funny sounds, scary sounds, surprises, etc. Perceptual learning about pitch height, dynamics, and timbre resulting from manual/aural exploration leads to further perceptual learning about the possibilities of tune building, or expressive function.

As well as the continual passive perceptual learning that goes on in a rich environment, there is also directed perceptual learning—the differentiation of attention that goes on when one person points out a distinction to another, or deliberately puts an individual in a situation designed to elicit perceptual learning. In the xylophone example, an adult might encourage or direct the child to try out certain actions and to pay attention to specific aspects of the resulting sounds. Aural training provides numerous examples of precisely this kind of process: an early skill in traditional aural training, for example, involves learning to recognize that a triad consists of three notes. Untrained listeners—and certainly children prior to training—tend to regard a chord as a single entity. This is a perfectly reasonable and "correct" perception: chords, and especially chords played on the piano, typically consist of notes with closely synchronized onsets, homogeneous timbres, and very similar dynamic levels—all of which help to produce fusion between the chord components, as Bregman (1990: 490–493) points out. So it is perfectly appropriate to hear a triadic chord as a single "thing": it *is* a single thing. But when an instructor points out that this single thing can also be heard to consist of a number of components, he or she is directing the learner's attention to a feature that was always available in the stimulus information but was previously undetected. Awareness of this information is nearly always achieved by a perception/action cycle: the learner is encouraged to "sing the middle note" or produce some other kind of overt action which has the effect of directing attention and consolidating the new perceptual awareness—a "reinforcement" of the perceptual information through the perception/action cycle. Thus the three factors discussed here (perception/action; adaptation; perceptual learning) explain how the resonance of a perceiver with its environment is not preordained or mysterious: a newborn infant (who, research increasingly reveals, has already had many weeks of prenatal perceptual learning; see Lecanuet 1996) has a limited range of powerful perceptual capacities and predispositions that give it a foothold in the world; but the overwhelming majority of an adult's more differentiated perception develops from these simple but powerful beginnings by virtue of environmental exposure/exploration and enculturation.

Ecology and Connectionism

One of the complaints that cognitivists make about the ecological approach is that it appears "magical." By rejecting the dominating role of internal representations, and with it the idea of explicit processing stages that are intended to explain perception and cognition, the ecological approach seems to retreat into a quasi-mystical belief that perception "just happens" as a result of a miraculous tuning of perceptual systems to the regularities of the environment. That charge is based on a fundamental misrepresentation of the ecological approach—one that completely ignores the central role of perceptual learning. The tuning of a perceiver's perceptual systems to the invariant properties of the environment is no happy accident, nor the result purely of some kind of Darwinian biological adaptation: it is a consequence of the flexibility of perception, and the plasticity of the nervous system, in the context of a shaping environment. Perceptual systems become attuned to the environment through continual exposure, both as the result of species adaptation on an evolutionary time scale, and as the consequence of perceptual learning within the lifetime of an individual.

But this still seems to beg the question: perceptual systems may be plastic, and the environment may be highly structured, but how does the shaping that is supposed to arise out of the interaction of the two actually take place? If internal representations and all of the mechanisms of a more standard cognitivist account are rejected, what is there instead? Having adjusted and adapted in some manner, in what sense does a perceiving organism actually perceive or know anything? And how does it ever know anything more than, or different from, the cumulative impact of the specific encounters with the environment that constitute its history? How can it ever generalize to novel situations, or be sensitive to certain aspects of the environment and not others?

One way to understand how this is possible is to consider connectionist models of perception—not as literal models of the actual structures and processes that may be involved, but rather as a relatively concrete "metaphor" for the ecological approach.[1] Despite a critique by Costall (1991), who argues that connectionism ignores the mutualism and evolving nature of the relationship between organism and environment, there are features of the approach that shed interesting light on ecological principles—however partial a representation the metaphor might in the end turn out to be.

Connectionist modeling, which was widely discussed in psychology and computer science following the publication of Rumelhart and McLelland's influential book *Parallel Distributed Processing* (Rumelhart and McLelland 1986), differentiates itself from traditional Artificial Intelligence (AI) by claiming that perceptual and cognitive processes can be modeled as the distributed property of a whole system, no particular part of which possesses any "knowledge" at all, rather than as the functioning of explicit rules operating on fixed storage addresses which contain representations or knowledge stores (a crude characterization of AI). A connectionist model typically consists of a network of nodes, interlinked with connections that can take variable values representing their strength (or weight). A layer of input units is connected to a layer of output units, with a variable number of "hidden layers" (usually no more than about two or three) in between. When input units are stimulated, a pattern of activation spreads through the network, the pattern depending on the structure of the connections and the weights assigned to them, and converging on a number of output units. Typically, the network is initially set up with random values assigned to the connection weights, so that the first "activation" results in random behavior of the system as a whole. Thereafter, the behavior of the system becomes more or less structured either on the basis of supervised learning, or according to a principle of self-organization. In supervised learning, the network is guided towards an intended final behavior by means of an explicit set of target values, provided by the experimenter/programmer. By contrast, in a self-organizing network, the final state of the system is not known in advance (although the experimenter/programmer will have an idea of the pattern of behavior that the network is supposed to model), and the system changes over time simply through repeated exposure to "stimulus" information (i.e. input).

Consider a connectionist approach to modeling two examples of musical behavior: listeners' preferences for simple melodies of various types and listeners' awareness of tonal functions.[2] Let us assume that for the first problem there are some data collected from a previous empirical study which show that for a particular collection of short unaccompanied melodies, listeners prefer those which start and finish on the same note, generally move in a stepwise manner, but contain at least two intervals of a major third or more. A network is then constructed that takes as its input the intervals between adjacent notes in each of the experimental melodies (since it is intervals rather than pitches that seem to determine preference), and has as its output a simple binary classification (like/dislike). The connections between the input units (sequences of intervals) and the output units (like/dislike), via some number of hidden layer units, are initially random—so that the first melody input will result in a response which is randomly "like" or "dislike," and therefore equally likely to be "correct" or "incorrect" in relation to the empirical data. In order to train the network by means of supervised learning, the network's correct responses (i.e. responses that conform to the empirical data) are reinforced by adjusting the connection weights between the input units and the output units. Incorrect responses are inhibited by changing the connection weights (increasing or decreasing them as appropriate) so as to steer the system towards the target relationship between input and output. In this way, over a period of supervised training that makes use of a subset of the melodies from the empirical study, the network becomes more and more differentiated in relation to its originally randomly organized state, as it is "shaped" by the supervisor.

At some point this training phase finishes, and the behavior of the system is then observed in relation to a number of melodies from the original set that have *not* so far been used. If the structure of the network and the principles on which it is based are appropriate, and the training period has been sufficient in terms of the number and variety of melodies presented, the network should now be able to classify these new melodies, employing the same general principles, in a way that mimics the preferences of the listeners on which the model is based. Melodies that listeners liked should activate the corresponding "like" output unit in the model, and melodies that the listeners disliked should activate the "dislike" unit.

In this imagined example, supervised learning seems appropriate because the experimenter/programmer knows in advance about listeners' preferences and is trying to train a network to exhibit those same preferences in order then to explore how well they generalize. It is essentially analogous to what happens when a rather prescriptive music teacher instructs a class about the differences between well-formed and ill-formed melodies, by playing them simple tunes and asking the students to judge whether each one is "good" or "bad," and providing feedback (i.e. the "right" answer) after each example. After a while, the expectation would be that the students might be able to generalize their classifying abilities (assuming that the training had been based on principled behavior of some kind!) to new examples of simple tunes not taken from the training set. The same expectation (and the same proviso about principled behavior) can apply to a network.

The parallel between the model and an ecological approach is the implicit manner in which both the human listeners, and the equivalent network, acquire their skills. Listeners asked to make preference judgments of the kind described here generally do not have explicit knowledge of how they make them, and in the same way the connectionist model described here[3] has neither been instructed with, nor does it contain, any explicit rules, and contains no explicit processing stages or knowledge representations. The adapted behavior arises out of a process of shaping, the effect of which is distributed throughout the network and is only seen when the network engages with its "environment"—in this case an environment consisting only of sequences of melodic intervals and "like" or "dislike" responses.

Using similar distributed principles, self-organizing networks arrive at some kind of "solution," or structured behavior, without any kind of explicit instruction. As empirical studies have shown, suitably encultured listeners can make systematic judgments about tonal structure in music (expressed, for instance, in terms of the perceived completeness or stability of a sequence) without any experience of "supervised learning" or formal music instruction (see e.g. Krumhansl 1990). The belief is that people become attuned to this property of music through simple exposure, due to the interaction of the regularities of the tonal environment with certain fundamental perceptual capacities of the auditory system. A variety of self-organizing methods have been explored in the connectionist literature to model this kind of unsupervised or "passive" learning, particularly those proposed by Kohonen (1984) and Grossberg (1982), which depend in one way or another on what is known as "competitive learning." The basic idea of competitive learning is that an existing connection (which may have been made fortuitously) is strengthened every time the connection is reiterated, while adjacent ("competing") connections are weakened. The consequence of this is that regularities in the environment progressively shape the network simply by virtue of their recurrence and co-dependence. If certain combinations of environmental events occur more frequently than others, then the corresponding connections in the network will become increasingly heavily weighted, and adjacent connections will become attenuated.

In a series of publications, Bharucha (1987; 1991a; 1991b; 1999; Bharucha and Todd 1991) has presented and developed a connectionist model for the perception of tonal harmony, as also has Leman (1991), using a slightly different (but nonetheless self-organizing) approach. Both Bharucha's and Leman's models take tonal material (notes or chords) as input, and give tonal interpretations, in the form of a dynamically changing sense of key, as output. In both cases, the networks start out in an essentially undifferentiated state, and by exposure to tonal materials develop tonally specific characteristics. These changes take place not because the networks acquire representations, or increase their memory content, but because their patterns of connectivity and consequent behavior as systems change: in other words, they adapt.

This relationship between adaptation and memory is tricky. Some authors (e.g. Crowder 1993) resist making the distinction by adopting a functionalist perspective: any system that behaves differently by virtue of past experience or exposure can be said to display memory. In common with Gibson (e.g. Gibson 1966: 275–278), I want to distinguish between memory proper, which involves the encoding, storage, and retrieval of previous events, and perceptual learning or environmental shaping, which is a sensitivity to current events, brought about by adaptation of the perceptual system to environmental invariants. To invoke "memory" on every occasion that an organism demonstrates a response to the environment that has been shaped by previous exposure leads to absurd consequences: the curious shapes of trees and bushes that grow in windy places, for instance, would have to be seen as "memories" of earlier windy interactions. This is manifestly wrong, and the more appropriate and familiar way to talk about such trees and bushes is in terms of growth: having grown in a particular way, under the influence of prevailing winds, they now interact with the wind in a specific manner. Neural networks can be regarded in the same light: having been exposed to environmental shaping (such as tonal chord sequences), the network has "grown" in a certain manner with the consequence that it behaves in a specific and differentiated fashion when it again "feels the wind" of the same or similar sequences blowing upon it. In the brain, this adaptive growth is referred to as plasticity (see Gregory 1987), and it is increasingly recognized as a fundamental and defining feature of the brain's functioning (e.g. Hurley and Noë 2003).

Changing the connection weights in a network model cannot be directly equated with changes in the connections (synapses) between neurons in the brain, but it is a reasonable approximation—or at the very least a metaphor for it. The sense of key in a tonal environment, or the identification of a characteristic motivic/harmonic procedure, both of which are temporally distributed properties, are behaviors that networks of this kind can be shown to demonstrate after suitable exposure. Once a network starts to behave in this way, it has in an ecological sense become attuned to the environment. If it is then exposed to a sufficiently similar musical sequence, it will enter into more or less the same state as before.[4] Reaching the same state as a result of exposure to the same (or similar) material is what recognition is—but at no point is a representation involved. The perceptual system has entered into a state that is "attuned" to the particular characteristics of the environment, and the state is one that the system has been in before. Recognition is that kind of perception for which the system has become adapted (or tuned).

The environmental events that gave rise to the particular connections and weightings in the system (or the synaptic links in the brain) are manifest relationships in the concrete physical world. The subsequent "tuning" of the network (whether artificial model or actual brain) is the result of exposure to those real events—their trace, or residue. That trace, and its reactivation, is experienced as a dynamic state of the network and thus a state of mind—an awareness of real-world relationships. When part of the original event sequence is encountered again (for example just the first two or three chords of a longer tonal sequence), the rest of the original dynamic state may be activated to greater or lesser extent—a principle that in psychology is called perceptual facilitation, or priming (e.g. Bharucha 1987; Bharucha and Stoeckig 1987), and which has been the subject of research in language, music and visual perception (e.g. Swinney 1979). Only some of the original events are present again on this occasion, so the meaning of the event, understood as the response of the whole network to the particular events that are present on this occasion, is achieved by virtue of the facilitated connections within the network that result from previous exposure. But these connections are only activated because of previous exposure: it is as though the network "relives" the real events even in their absence. It is the actual exposure to the original conditions, however, that gave rise to the connections in the first place, and if nothing like those material conditions were ever to be encountered again, then eventually the facilitated connections would disappear too. The "noise" in a connectionist network (a constant background of random activation, exacerbated by the atrophying of weak connections by competitive learning) means that to be maintained, structured connections need to be reactivated or reinforced from time to time. Fundamentally, then, the whole system depends on, but is not reducible to, the effects of exposure to real-world events. As Gibson (1966) put it: "all knowledge rests on sensitivity" (26).

Invariants in Perception

From the point of view of adaptation, an organism's most pressing need is to know "what is going on" in the environment. As a consequence, the ecological approach emphasizes the critical importance of information as information *for* something (objects and events). Perception is not a process of taking in "raw sensations" and then interpreting them, and the purely sensory character of perception is usually not at all evident to a perceiver. It is the objects and events that are specified in perception that are important: whether people notice a fire because they see the flames, hear the crackle, smell the smoke, or feel the heat is of little importance compared to the fact that they detect the event (the fire). When perception proceeds in an unproblematic way, we are usually unaware of the sensory aspect of the stimulus information, and are only attuned to the events that are specified by stimulus structure. But when that relationship is problematic, the stimulus structure itself can become more evident.

This can be the case with ambiguous or degraded perceptual information, as figure 1.1 is intended to illustrate. People who look at this image and see no recognizable scene (look at it now), tend

Figure 1.1   What do you see here? (Photographer: R. C. James).

to be much more aware of the array of differently shaped patches of black and white than those who immediately see a recognizable scene. The characteristics of the visual array (patches of black and white with certain shapes and orientations) are much more visible when you cannot see what the array specifies than when you see it as a picture of a Dalmatian dog. Similarly, a piece of music which presents sampled everyday sounds in a transformed, or radically de-contextualized, fashion may encourage a listener to detect the structure of the stimulus information (what might be called "purely sonorous" structures) by virtue of a disruption of the normal relationship of source specification (see Dibben 2001). Paradoxically, when a person hears what a sound means (i.e. understands the sound in relation to its source), it becomes more difficult to detect the sound's distinctive features. Speech perception provides a striking case of this: it is a common experience when listening to the sounds of an unfamiliar foreign language to notice the huge variety and specific qualities of the sounds that make up the language—to be quite acutely aware, in other words, of continuously variable acoustical features but to understand nothing. To a native speaker/listener, however, these are paradoxically far more difficult to detect even though they are the critical features that enable the language to function as a communicative medium at all.

Speech also demonstrates another very general characteristic of perception: the environment is usually perceived as comparatively stable despite widespread and continual physical variations. A native speaker/listener perceives the speech of others as being identifiable and comprehensible despite dramatic differences in the physical signals (vocal range, speed, accent, loudness, etc). How are the stability and constancy of the perceived environment to be explained? The key to this lies in the principle of invariance—the idea that within the continuous changes to which a perceiver is exposed there are also invariant properties. As the ecological approach emphasizes, these invariant properties are those of the stimulus information itself—not a representational projection by the perceiver. They are relationships between stimulus properties that remain unchanged despite transformations of the stimulus array as a whole. For example, a person hearing a passing motorbike will be exposed to a continuously changing array of acoustical information, but within that array there will be invariant acoustical properties, in a specific pattern of relationships, which together identify the motorbike and which remain constant under transformation (pitch changes due to the Doppler effect, amplitude change due to distance, etc). Warren and Verbrugge (1984), for example, showed that the sounds of objects bouncing and breaking could be distinguished from one another on the basis of the temporal properties of the impact sequences, and showed that listeners could still reliably distinguish between bouncing and breaking in artificially generated examples that used only a highly simplified simulation of the temporal properties of real impact sequences. The acoustical invariants that specify bouncing and breaking are, in other words, two different temporal patterns of impacts.

Music offers a particularly clear example of invariance in the perceived identity of material under transposition and other kinds of transformation. A theme or motif in music can be regarded as an invariant (a pattern of temporal proportions and pitch intervals) that is left intact, and hence retains its identity, under transformations such as pitch transposition or changes in global tempo. As Dowling and Harwood (1986) point out, these invariants can be of different orders, from local and specific to more general:

> Some invariants are specific to a certain piece, such as the pitch and rhythm contour of the initial theme of Beethoven's Fifth Symphony. Other invariants heard in a particular piece are common to a large family of similar pieces, for example, the characteristic repeated rhythmic pattern of certain dances such as beguine and tango. In terms of scale-structure invariants, a piece may exhibit a particular shift between keys in the middle. . . . Such a pattern involves variation within the single piece, but if the listener has heard many such pieces with the same pattern of modulation, then that pattern constitutes an invariant that the listener can perceive in each piece he or she hears, even pieces not heard before. Such invariants across sets of pieces constitute what we mean by a style. (Dowling and Harwood 1986: 160–161)

Notice the implicit reference to perceptual learning: listeners become more attuned to the invariants that specify a style, or a particular harmonic invariant (e.g. tonic/dominant alternation) through exposure to a particular repertoire, whether that exposure is accompanied by direct instruction or not. But notice also that these higher order invariants are no more abstract than the most

specific and local invariant that is unique to one particular context, even if some of them may be more extended in time: in every
case the invariant is a set of relationships that is available in the
stimulus information. The ecological approach resists the cognitive tendency to explain constancy and invariance in terms of internal processes and points to the environmental and "given" nature
of the phenomenon.

Affordance

The idea of invariants leads to another important concept that
Gibson developed, that of "affordance," which relates directly
to the central theme of this book—musical meaning. Here is the
passage in *The Senses Considered as Perceptual Systems* where Gibson
introduces the term:

> When the constant properties of constant objects are
> perceived (the shape, size, color, texture, composition,
> motion, animation, and position relative to other objects),
> the observer can go on to detect their *affordances*. I have
> coined this word as a substitute for *values*, a term which
> carries an old burden of philosophical meaning. I mean
> simply what things furnish, for good or ill. What they
> *afford* the observer, after all, depends on their properties.
> The simplest affordance, as food, for example, or as a
> predatory enemy, may well be detected without learning
> by the young of some animals, but in general learning is
> all-important for this kind of perception. The child learns
> what things are manipulable and how they can be manipu-
> lated, what things are hurtful, what things are edible, what
> things can be put together with other things or put inside
> other things—and so on without limit. He also learns what
> objects can be used as the means to obtain a goal, or to
> make other desirable objects, or to make people do what

he wants them to do. In short, the human observer learns to detect what have been called the values or meanings of things, perceiving their distinctive features, putting them into categories and subcategories, noticing their similarities and differences and even studying them for their own sakes, apart from learning what to do about them. All this discrimination, wonderful to say, has to be based entirely on the education of his attention to the subtleties of invariant stimulus information. (Gibson 1966: 285)

In this definition of affordance, Gibson places considerable emphasis on the properties of objects themselves, and some authors (e.g. Noble 1991) have criticized Gibson for having a rigid and one-sided approach. Elsewhere in his writing, however, Gibson presents the concept in a much more dialectical or mutual fashion, pointing out that although affordances depend on the properties of the object they don't depend solely on them: affordances are the product both of objective properties and the capacities and needs of the organism that encounters them.

> The verb *to afford* is found in the dictionary, but the noun *affordance* is not. I have made it up. I mean by it something that refers to both the environment and the animal in a way that no existing term does. It implies the complementarity of the animal and the environment. (Gibson 1979: 122; emphasis in original)

As Flach and Smith (2000) point out, Gibson's noun ("affordance") threatens to reify an essentially dynamic concept, so there may be advantages in sticking with the verb. To a person, a wooden chair affords sitting, while to a termite it affords eating. Equally, the same chair affords self-defense to a person under attack—an illustration of the way in which an organism can notice different affordances according to its own changing needs. The relationship is neither a case of organisms imposing their needs on an indifferent environment, nor a fixed environment determining possibilities: to a person, a chair can afford sitting and self-defense, but simply cannot afford eating because of the relationship between the capabilities of the human digestive system and the properties of wood. Note that the principle of affordance does not imply that perception will always be obvious and unambiguous, since objects and events can give rise to more than one perceptual experience. If perceptual information "carries different or contradictory variables of information it will afford different or contradictory perceptual experiences" (Gibson 1966: 248).

Although Gibson writes here of perceptual experience as an affordance, elsewhere in his writing and in the writing of other eco-logical psychologists, affordances are primarily understood as the *action* consequences of encountering perceptual information in the world. A chair affords sitting, a stick affords throwing, raspberries afford eating, a sharp pencil affords writing. In many ways, music fits into this scheme unproblematically: music affords dancing, worship, co-ordinated working, persuasion, emotional catharsis, marching, foot-tapping, and a myriad other activities of a perfectly tangible kind. But in certain musical traditions (and the con-cert music of the West is an obvious example) listening to music has become somewhat divorced from overt action—has become apparently autonomous. The particular consequences of these specific circumstances are examined elsewhere in this book (chap-ter 5 and the conclusion), but the example highlights the social nature of affordances for human beings. A concentration on com-mon or garden objects might lead to the erroneous conclusion that affordances are a simple matter of physical properties and percep-tual capacities. But even the most cursory consideration of some more socially embedded objects demonstrates the importance of the social component. A violin, for example, affords burning, but social factors ensure that this is a rather remote affordance—which might only be realized in extreme circumstances or by an individual who had no regard for (or even deliberately disdained) the musical context which regulates its affordances.[5]

Nature and Culture

The perspective offered so far implies an environment consisting of sources of information that are all of the same general kind. But can the sound of horses' hooves, the sound of a radio commentary on a horse race, the sound of Tennyson's poem "The Charge of the Light Brigade," and the sound of Wagner's "Valkyries" leitmotiv really be regarded as equivalent sources of information about horses? Can a single approach deal with a whole range of more or less culturally mediated information sources? Gibson himself wrote of the need to avoid a sharp division between culture and nature—and in doing so made one of his rare references to music:

> In the study of anthropology and ecology, the 'natural' environment is often distinguished from the 'cultural' environment. As described here, there is no sharp division between them. Culture evolved out of natural opportunities. The cultural environment, however, is often divided into two parts, 'material' culture and 'non-material' culture. This is a seriously misleading distinction, for it seems to imply that language, tradition, art, music, law, and religion are immaterial, insubstantial, or intangible, whereas tools, shelters, clothing, vehicles, and books are not. Symbols are taken to be profoundly different from things. But let us be clear about this. There have to be modes of stimulation, or ways of conveying information, for any individual to perceive anything, however abstract. He must be sensitive to stimuli no matter how universal or fine-spun the thing he apprehends. No symbol exists except as it is realized in sound, projected light, mechanical contact, or the like. (Gibson 1966: 26)

Once a convention or tradition is established and is embodied in widespread and relatively permanent objects and practices, it becomes as much a part of the environment as any other feature. As

Heft (2001) and Windsor (1995; 2000) have pointed out, cultural regularities are as much a part of the environment as natural forces, and they exert their influence on the invariants of the world in just the same way.

It is important to recognize the cultural specificity of perception, but since for human beings *every* circumstance and experience is cultural, there is no basis on which to propose some kind of primary pre-cultural experience characterized by a spurious immediacy. The theoretically arbitrary nature of linguistic and other semiotic codes is largely irrelevant to the way in which they function once a system and community are established: once embedded in a system, they are subject to enormous systematic inertia and cannot simply be overturned at a moment's notice. Although arbitrary in principle, they take on a fixed character in practice.

> The association of sound and representation is the outcome of a collective training (for instance the learning of the French tongue); this association—which is the signification—is by no means arbitrary (for no French person is free to modify it), indeed it is, on the contrary, necessary. . . . We shall therefore say in general terms that in the language the link between the signifier and signified is contractual in its principle, but that this contract is collective, inscribed in a long temporality (Saussure says that 'a language is always a legacy'), and that consequently it is, as it were, *naturalized*; in the same way, Levi-Strauss specified that the linguistic sign is arbitrary *a priori* but non-arbitrary *a posteriori*. (Barthes 1968: 50–51; emphasis in original)

The same set of principles, therefore, can account for the ways in which perceivers pick up information from all parts of the environment—cultural and natural. When I hear someone explaining that the "Valkyries" leitmotiv is just one example of a "horse" topic in music, the vocal sounds may specify an adult male speaker from Scotland, who is animated and enthusiastic, is standing about two meters away from me and facing me, and is telling me about horses, rhythm, and the history of musical materials. The sounds specify the speaker's sex by virtue of pitch and timbral features that are the direct consequence of the size and shape of a man's vocal tract (a natural consequence), even as a portion of these same sounds also specify the word "topic," which in turn denotes a particular concept by virtue of a cultural (linguistic) convention.

Perception and Cognition

A consideration of language demonstrates the close relationship between perception and cognition. Because of its emphasis on understanding perception, the ecological approach in general, and Gibson in particular, have been accused of having no theory of cognition—or even of rejecting cognition altogether. As Reed (1988; 1991; 1996) has shown in Gibson's own writings, and has argued from more general ecological principles, nothing could be further from the truth. Gibson's own aim was to develop a cognitive psychology—but one which theorized perception in a radically different manner from the information-processing approach and also expressed the relationship between perception and cognition quite differently. Despite the incorporation of "top-down" and "bottom-up" interactions, overlapping stages of processing, and so on, the standard cognitive approach is to regard perception as simply the starting-point for a series of cognitive processes—the information-gathering that precedes the real business of sorting out and structuring the data into a representation of some kind. Perception starts when stimuli cause sensations, according to this view, and all the rest is cognitive processing of one sort or another.

The ecological approach presents the situation entirely differently because it rejects the whole idea of "stimuli" in perception. Perceiving organisms seek out and respond to perceptual information that specifies objects and events in the environment, and this perceiving is a continuous process that is both initiated by, and results in, action.[6] One consequence of recognizing perception as a process is that, while mainstream psychology presents the temporal aspect of perception as a stream of discrete stimuli, processed separately and "glued together" by memory, an ecological approach sees it as perceptual flow—the specification of objects and events over time. There is nothing more problematic in principle about temporal successiveness than spatial adjacency in the distribution of perceptual information. Some of Gibson's early research was concerned with investigating the perceptual flow that specified the horizon (or the point of touchdown) as pilots landed aeroplanes (Gibson 1958), and a considerable amount of subsequent research has shown the importance of both optic and acoustic flow in a variety of perceptual tasks with humans and other animals (e.g. Lee 1980; Warren and Verbrugge 1984).

The relationship between perception and cognition is, for Gibson and most other ecological psychologists, bound up with the distinction between direct and indirect forms of knowing. In his 1966 book, Gibson wrote:

> In this book, a distinction will be made between perceptual cognition, or knowledge of the environment, and symbolic cognition, or knowledge *about* the environment. The former is a direct response to things based on stimulus information, the latter is an indirect response to things based on stimulus sources produced by another human individual. The information in the latter case is *coded*; in the former case it cannot properly be called that. (Gibson 1966: 91; emphasis in original)

Representational systems have particular properties that go beyond their purely perceptual attributes: language, for instance, has the property of semantics that gives it the possibilities of predication and discursiveness—the capacity to articulate and communicate *about* something. It can be used to provide knowledge of abstract concepts (the idea of eternity), and of objects and events that are elsewhere (the layout of the surface of the moon), or in the future (tomorrow's weather)—none of which can be perceived (or not at this time and place). When we learn about something by virtue of a representational system of some kind (language, maps, road signs, etc.), we learn not by virtue of what the perceptual information directly specifies, but because what is specified in turn stands for something conceptual, and this conceptual content both adds to our experience and helps to guide our subsequent perception. If I read about the layout of the surface of the moon, this not only informs me about it: it also helps me to perceive and navigate it if I subsequently arrive there. Gibson writes of the ways in which "Perceiving helps talking, and talking fixes the gains of perceiving" (Gibson 1966: 282), though what people come to know about the world through representational systems can, of course, be completely at odds with what they discover through a direct perceptual encounter. I might read about a thrilling-sounding roller-coaster ride, only to find that I hate it when I actually have a go.

We live in a world permeated by representational systems, but it would be wrong to conclude that all of human experience therefore consists of symbolic cognition. Representational systems can guide perceptual information pick-up explicitly or tacitly, and can lead to the accumulation and transformation of knowledge, but every kind of knowing rests upon or involves a perceptual relationship with the environment. In the specific case of music, the relationship between these different ways of knowing has been widely debated (e.g. Cook 1990; 1994; 1998; Kerman 1985; Nattiez 1990; Scruton 1997). The construction of musical meaning through language and other forms of representation is undeniable, but it does not proceed independently of the affordances of musical materials. Ideologies and discourses, however powerful or persuasive they may seem to be, cannot simply impose themselves arbitrarily on the perceptual sensitivities of human beings, which are rooted in (though not defined by) the common ground of immediate experience.

Three More Sound Examples

Consider now three more imagined sound clips like those discussed at the start of the introduction—tracks on an unlabeled recording. Imagine that the first consists of the sounds of a violin being tuned. What do these sounds specify—or rather (and this amounts to the same question) what is their perceptual meaning? Presented like this, the question is unanswerable, since the perceiver is unspecified and, as already discussed, the ecological position rests on the premise that perceptual specification is a reciprocal relationship between the invariants of the environment and the particular capacities of the perceiver. Let us assume, therefore, that the listener presupposed in the discussion of the three following examples is a person enculturated in mainstream classical and pop music of the Western tradition, with roughly the aural awareness and technical understanding of a university music student. Each example is played over a hi-fi, the listener is asked to say what he or she hears, and let us suppose that the response to this first one is "someone tuning a violin." Notice that this description of the perceptual meaning of the sound (or what the sound specifies) refers to a number of different kinds of object or event: there is the instrument (violin), presumably specified by invariants such as the timbre, pitch height, and attack characteristics, which also specify the mode of activation (bowing) of the instrument and thus help to signal both its identity and the presence of a human being. Then there is the particular kind of event (*tuning* the instrument) that is specified in the stimulus invariants—just as the instrument itself is. In this case the invariants would include the irregular, nonmetrical rhythm of the bow strokes; the consistent sounding of only open strings (specified by their characteristic timbre) at intervals of approximately a perfect fifth, always in pairs sounded together; and the continuous pitch glides in just one of the two paired strings that bring the pitches nearer to, or further from, a perfect fifth. Changing any of these invariants has the potential to cause the sound to specify a quite different musical event: if the two pitches, for instance, both varied in a continuous gliding manner in perfect parallelism, the resulting sounds might be heard as specifying a person playing or practicing a passage of *music* of some kind. This is a significantly different kind of event from the culturally specific phenomenon of "tuning," which in the Western classical system has a particular cultural value, lying as it does outside the boundary of a "piece of music."[7] It would be a straightforward matter to investigate the precise nature of the invariants that specify "tuning a violin" by modifying each of the invariant dimensions (rhythmic irregularity, interval structure, pitch glides, timbre) mentioned here—and any others that turned out to be important. And it is also clear that what is specified is both material and concrete (an instrument, a body, a class of action) and also social: tuning an instrument is a socially defined practice, with a distinct place in the cultural system of Western concert music.

Now imagine another example with the same general conditions—this time a recording of a perfect cadence in F played on the piano. Our assumed listener might give a variety of answers to the question, "What do you hear?" depending on his or her specific skills. Among such answers might be: "a musical ending"; "an extract from an aural test"; "a cadence played on the piano"; "a perfect cadence in F played on the piano." The response given would depend on the listener's descriptive competence, current preoccupations, and particular perceptual capacities: the last response would only be possible (given the circumstances) for a person with absolute pitch. But the four possibilities (and there are of course many more) demonstrate once again the direct pick-up of a very concrete material source (the piano) and an equally direct quality that is often regarded as far more abstract—a tonal function (closure, cadence), or a social function (the testing of aural skills). These are quite obviously socially defined events—a musical function that arises out of the operation of a musical system, or a training function that arises out of an educational system—but they are nonetheless directly specified in the sounds themselves to a suitably attuned perceiver. Again it is not difficult to envisage straightforward empirical studies that could determine what the invariants that specify "cadence" or "aural test" might be (harmonic, rhythmic, textural, etc.).

As a final example, imagine a one-second burst from the middle of the tenor aria "La donna e mobile" from Verdi's opera *Rigoletto*—the kind of sound clip that you might get if you were scanning the stations on an analogue radio, and happened to pass through a broadcast of that opera. Again a range of responses to the question, "What do you hear?" might be imagined from the type of listener defined above: "vocal music"; "a burst of opera"; "over-the-top singing"; "an extract from Verdi's *Rigoletto*." These again represent different perceptual capacities in some sense, as well as different musical values and kinds of musical experience. "Over-the-top singing" might be the response of someone whose previous experience was primarily of genres other than opera, who had sufficient exposure to this kind of singing to be attuned to its general type, but who had little interest in it or sympathy with it. All of the responses however, are consistent with the idea that auditory information can specify what may be regarded as abstract events—and certainly events that are overwhelmingly culturally defined.

Summary

This chapter has challenged those information-processing accounts of music perception that imply, or assert, that the cultural and ideological components of music are more abstract and remote than are its basic sensory and perceptual attributes, and that it is to the latter that listeners primarily respond. The ecological approach to perception offers an alternative view that gives a coherent account of the directness of listeners' perceptual responses to a variety of environmental attributes, ranging from the spatial location and physical source of musical sounds, to their structural function and cultural and ideological value. This entails extending ecological theory into the cultural environment, based on the principle that the material objects and practices that constitute culture are just as directly specified in the auditory invariants of music as the events and objects of the natural environment are specified in their corresponding auditory information. The conventions of culture, arbitrary though they may be in principle, are in practice as binding as a natural law. The directness of our perception of the world is not an inexplicable or "magical" reciprocity between perceiver and environment: it is the consequence of adaptation, perceptual learning, and the interdependence of perception and action. The advantages of this approach as far as music is concerned are that it places the emphasis on an investigation of the invariants that specify all of the phenomena that music is able to afford in relation to the diversity of perceptual capacities of different listeners; and that it offers a framework within which attributes of music that have previously been regarded as poles apart (from physical sources and musical structures to cultural meaning and critical content) can be understood together. This last point is based on a principle that recognizes the distinctiveness of different phenomena and the manner in which they may be specified, as well as the reciprocity between listeners' capacities and environmental opportunities (affordances), while asserting the commonality of the perceptual principles on which a sensitivity to these phenomena depends.

2 ∼

Jimi Hendrix's "Star Spangled Banner"

The previous chapter presented the theoretical basis of an ecological approach to music perception, discussing it in relation to some imagined brief sound examples. The purpose of this chapter is to show how the approach might work with a more extended and real musical example: Jimi Hendrix's performance of "The Star Spangled Banner" at the Woodstock festival in 1969.

Hendrix's performance at Woodstock, an emblem of the hippie movement of the 1960s, has become a classic moment in the history of musical protest against the United States' war in Vietnam. Commentaries (e.g. Dempster 1994) have pointed to the ways in which Hendrix used the guitar to represent the sounds of modern warfare but have had little more to say about the sounds of the performance other than to comment on this mimetic quality. My approach in this chapter is to regard the recorded performance as a wordless piece of musical critique that provides an opportunity to demonstrate the way in which an ecological approach can tackle the diverse components of the music's meaning and impact. The performance can be heard on Polydor CD 517 235-2 *Jimi Hendrix: The Ultimate Experience.* It is a live recording—essentially a free and unmetered guitar solo for Hendrix, underpinned by the drums and bass. The melody of the anthem emerges out of high guitar feedback and is then played on the guitar more or less literally as far as the pitches are concerned for the first four phrases (to 0:32) and their repeat (to 1:06), although with increasing amounts of pitch bending and embellishment.[1] The sound in both of these first two large phrases is characterized, however, by the constant threat of feedback that is only just kept under control, a high level of distortion, and the swirling spatial effects of playing through Leslie loudspeakers.[2] The second section of the theme (from 1:10) disintegrates into feedback and roaring swoops of sound up and down the guitar. The rest of the performance (which lasts for a total of about four minutes) consists of a mixture of dense, distorted guitar sound and feedback, with sudden patches of clarity when the outlines of the melody can be heard continuing—as if the anthem is rising up through clouds of sound. Finally, just as the conclusion to the anthem is engulfed once again, it is transformed into the opening of "Purple Haze"—Hendrix's own signature tune. A schematic transcription of the performance is given in example 2.1 to provide a reference "map" for subsequent discussion. Example 2.2 gives the score and words for the first verse of the anthem, again for reference and to provide a comparison with Hendrix's performance.

The performance, which took place against the background of the Vietnam War, has been described in the following terms:

> The ironies were murderous: a black man with a white guitar; a massive, almost exclusively white audience wallowing in a paddy field of its own making; the clear, pure, trumpet-like notes of the familiar melody struggling to pierce through clouds of tear-gas, the explosions of cluster-bombs, the screams of the dying, the crackle of the flames, the heavy palls of smoke stinking with human grease, the hovering of helicopters. . . . One man with a guitar said more in three and a half minutes about that peculiarly disgusting war and its reverberations than all the novels, memoirs and movies put together. (Murray, cited in Martin 1995: 262–263)

Example 2.1   Transcription of Jimi Hendrix's performance of
"The Star Spangled Banner."

Example 2.2   Score of the first verse and chorus of
"The Star Spangled Banner."

Murray hears the performance as a strikingly critical and subversive rendering of the American national anthem, but he leaves unexplored how it is that the sounds have this impact, or what it is in the performance that delivers this critique. A sceptic might argue that there is nothing in the sounds themselves that justifies his interpretation, and that the power of the performance derives from a combination of the circumstances and visual spectacle of the performance, and Murray's own projection—a projection generated by his desire to portray Hendrix as a cultural radical, and his music as the nonverbal expression of radical America's conscience. By contrast, my analysis attempts to show that the impact of the performance can be traced to properties that are specified in the sounds themselves, although there is undoubtedly more than one way to hear these sounds. As the imaginary sound examples of chapter 1 demonstrated, an ecological approach recognizes that even comparatively simple sounds can afford more than one interpretation—and aesthetic objects are deliberately structured so as to exploit this polyvalence. But this in no way undermines an ecological stance: rather, it encourages a detailed and ecologically appropriate examination of the stimulus invariants and the kinds of sources that they may specify in relation to the sensitivities of the perceiver(s) in question.[3]

The Performance

Given the particular focus on listening in this book, my analysis will consider the performance as it is presented on CD, rather than the experience of the live performance (or the film of it) to which Murray clearly refers in the extract above. Thus no access to knowledge of white guitars, the ethnicity of the audience, or the physical context of the performance is assumed in what follows,[4] though of course there is no attempt to "bracket out" the knowledge that a suitably enculturated listener with normal access to the CD cover would have—including the information that this is a performance by Jimi Hendrix, that "The Star Spangled Banner" is the American national anthem, or that this is rock music.

The performance starts on the recording with a fade-in to a high $G5$ pitch that is arguably of indeterminate instrumental origin for a couple of seconds or so: it is hard to be sure what source is specified by this sound. The reason (and within another second or two it becomes clear) is that the sound specifies controlled guitar feedback—a very characteristic sound, but one that is instrumentally paradoxical since it comes from an instrument that is usually activated by plucking, and thus by recognizable attack points and relatively steep onsets. During feedback, however, the instrument produces sounds that have no definable attack point (they grow rather gradually out of the sympathetic vibration of one or more strings exposed to a nearby loudspeaker) and which have a tendency to change pitch (along the harmonic series) in a somewhat unpredictable manner. The onset characteristics and subsequent behavior of these guitar sounds are therefore quite unlike those of the instrument played in a more conventional manner—but have nonetheless become a readily identifiable sound and technique in rock music. At around 0:03 the sounds of a drum kit[5] begin to become audible as well, and the generic context within which this performance is contained is now clearly specified: after an indeterminate start, the instrumentation specifies the genre of rock music, and furthermore, by about 0:04 when the sounds of a large audience clapping and cheering are audible, it is also evident that this is a live performance.

As example 2.1 shows, the feedback sounds are soon "reined-in" and subordinated to more conventionally produced notes on the guitar (at 0:07); the first six notes outline the descending and then ascending arpeggio, with its characteristic rhythmic profile, that specifies the opening of the American national anthem. An index of the strength with which this pattern of pitch and rhythm specifies the anthem (at least to the audience present at the live performance) is the clearly audible cheer of recognition that greets only the second or third note of this opening phrase. The sounds of this solo guitar are, however, not perceptually straightforward. By the sixth note (E4 at 0:10) the swirling and dynamically varying quality of the sound is apparent, and seems paradoxically to specify both an unstable physical location and one whose instability is somehow controlled (by virtue of the regularity of the effect). As already explained, this is a consequence of the Leslie loudspeakers through which the guitar is played, since their fixed rotational speed results in a regular but musically arbitrary fluctuation in dynamic level and timbre.

The performance has a recitative-like character in the way that it preserves the basic rhythmic outline of the material, but does so in discontinuous blocks separated by unmeasured pauses or extensions. The rhythmic proportions are sufficiently clear (particularly in the first five notes, and indeed the great majority of the first eight-bar phrase) to preserve the identity of the anthem, but enormous liberties are taken with the length of individual notes: the sixth note (E4 at 0:10), for instance, lasts about twice as long as it should (at the tempo established by the first two or three notes). Other similar examples are E4 at 0:36, B3 at 0:45, and G#4 at 0:52. Taken together, these expressive distortions of the anthem's rhythmic structure specify the improvisational character of the performance—the performer is playing *with* the anthem rather than playing it.

In the same way, the increasing amount of melodic embellishment that adorns the performance as it proceeds specifies the performer's freedom to do what he will with the material, and to assimilate it to a genre (rock) that is in opposition to the anthem's conventional cultural position. In simple terms, national anthems (like flags and coats of arms), as the emblems of nationhood, stand for the cultural status quo and are expected to remain unchanging and inviolate, while the rock music of this period is predominantly countercultural and associated with the constant change that is the consequence of a fundamentally performance-based (as opposed to text-based) and improvisatory musical tradition. A small feature of the performance that occurs early on, and which is then elaborated, is significant in making this clash of values apparent: the seventh note (G#4) at 0:14 is approached by a small but clearly audible pitch bend or glide up to the note from the preceding E4—a characteristic stylistic invariant for rock-guitar playing. Among increasing numbers of these invariants, three particularly obvious examples are the trilling embellishment of G#4 and F#4 at 0:39–0:41; the D#4, C#4, B3 elaboration of B3 at 0:4–0:49 that uses progressively more feedback; and most salient of them all, the huge pitch bend down from G#4 towards E4 that occurs at 0:51–0:55. At the same time as the anthem is specified by its intervallic and rhythmic invariants, rock as a genre is specified by invariants of performance. The cultural clash is directly specified in the material itself.

The second part of the anthem (bar 8, "And the rockets' red glare"; see example 2.2) starts reasonably straight, but following the note corresponding to the word "glare" at 1:10, the performance suddenly breaks out of this relatively disciplined and faithful rendering of the anthem (from the point of view of pitches and rhythms), and becomes essentially unrecognizable: a passage of dramatic and violent guitar sounds roar and swoop around the instrument for the next 30 seconds. In the language of ecological acoustics, these sounds have a high level of distortion—inharmonic or aperiodic (noise) components, largely indeterminate pitches (though example 2.1 indicates that there are moments when more distinguishable pitches do emerge), no recognizable rhythmic structure, and pitch trajectories which specify large, rapid, and violent physical gestures on the guitar. When identifiable pitches do emerge, they tend to fall into two relatively distinct classes: pitches somewhere in the region of G#3 and E3, which provide a tenuous tonal continuity with the anthem, and pitches in a continuous pitch region between F5 and G5 that specify some kind of pitch contrast (see example 2.1). The opposition between these two is emphasized by the large registral gulf between them, and the dramatic timbral difference: while the low pitches around E3 are growly and dense, the pitches around F5 to G5 are clearer and far more focused, but in a state of constant pitch bend—more like a wail or siren than the discrete pitches of instrumental music. The whole passage, then, specifies the dissolution, engulfment, or destruction of all that has been established previously. Noise, as Eno (1996: 195) observes, has a particular kind of power in rock music:

Distortion and complexity are the sources of noise. Rock music is built on distortion: on the idea that things are enriched, not degraded, by noise. To allow something to become noisy is to allow it to support multiple readings. It is a way of multiplying resonances.

It is also a way of 'making the medium fail'—thus giving the impression that what you are doing is bursting out of the material: 'I'm too big for this medium.'

Out of this dense noisiness the guitar suddenly emerges at 1:41 with six notes from the second half of the anthem (from the quaver upbeats to bar 11 to the first note of bar 12—the words of the anthem here being "the bombs bursting in air"; see example 2.2). They are played with a hard and focused timbre and much sharper attack points—a disjunction with what preceded them that seems to specify an almost palpably physical relationship. In an everyday circumstance, this type of change of sound and material might specify the sudden emergence of one object from behind or underneath another, or an object or person rising above and out of dense and potentially engulfing surroundings, or the sudden cessation of chaotic events, revealing the continued presence of a more structured and predictable object. It is in these properties that the connection with Murray's description (above) of the performance as "the clear, pure, trumpet-like notes of the familiar melody struggling to pierce through clouds of tear-gas, the explosions of cluster-bombs, the screams of the dying, the crackle of the flames, the heavy palls of smoke stinking with human grease, the hovering of helicopters" may be made—although the specificity of the objects and events of war that he invokes are difficult to justify in terms of the invariants of the performance.[6]

The six notes of this sudden emergence, however, are almost immediately displaced or engulfed again by the chaos from which they emerged. This happens in two ways: first at 1:44 by the disruptive sound of two alternating pitches at an interval of a tritone (B♭/E; see example 2.1), which retain the instrumental and discrete pitch character of the theme but undermine it in terms of tonal implications and tonal stability; and then with a resumption (at around 1:49) of the noisy and chaotic sounds that were heard before. Following one or two more pitched fragments at around 2:15–2:20, the guitar again emerges with a clear and identifiably pitched sound at 2:27, playing bars 13 to 16 of the anthem as if the preceding three-quarters of a minute of noise and chaos had come from some quite different world.

Starting at 2:42, there is a passage that presents a somewhat different kind of "destruction of material" from those that have gone before—one which is much more closely tied to a more conventional notion of musical material. Having reached E_5 at 2:42 from two upbeat B_4 quavers (as if starting the chorus at "O, say, does that . . ."), the melody now drops back to B_4 and rises up again through E_5 to $G\#_5$ forming an arpeggiation in E major which is now simply repeated three times in immediate succession, using a clear guitar sound—though in a high register and with a kind of charge and tension in the sound that suggests that it might break up at any moment into feedback and dissolution. The destruction here is the undoing of the recognizable and specific melody (the invariants of the American national anthem) into undifferentiated tonal material that specifies no *particular* melody at all—a kind of musical undoing that is as negating of the anthem as any of the more violent transformations and interventions that preceded it. This is what I heard as a (British) listener.

But an anonymous American listener/reader who wrote to me heard something quite different here—and was astonished that I had *not* heard it: what I had heard as undifferentiated arpeggiation, the American heard as the bugle call known as "Taps," or "Day is Done," used as the lights-out call at camp and also—and much more significantly—as the final bugle call at military funerals. At the time, many American listeners would have heard it played during the nationally televised Kennedy funerals, as well as in any number of World War II films.[7] Its reference in Hendrix's performance to the death of American soldiers in Vietnam, and perhaps more generally to the death of the "American dream," would have been loud and clear for many in the Woodstock audience. The contrast between my original hearing of this passage as a dissolution into nonspecific material, and this far more specific hearing of the same passage by an American listener nicely illustrates the ecological principle of mutualism: the same three-note pitch pattern in Hendrix's performance specifies a bugle call to my American informant and an undifferentiated arpeggio to me. I hear this as "dissolution" of a certain kind, the American listener hears it as some kind of requiem. And now, of course, having had this reference pointed out to me, and having heard "Taps" enough times to know what this listener/reader means, I too hear the funereal quality of this passage—an example of the way in which language can steer a perceiver towards specific invariants (in this case culturally specific invariants) in a complex signal.[8]

At 2:50 the guitar resumes its middle register again and takes up the chorus ("O, say, does that Star-Spangled Banner yet wave," bars 17–20), rhythmically and melodically somewhat altered. It is at first disrupted by a tremolando on every note, which then disappears (at 3:00) as arbitrarily as it appeared, leaving the melody hanging on a long intensifying D#4 with wide vibrato and increasing amounts of feedback. Until the feedback really takes hold, this D#4 strongly suggests that the music will come to some kind of cadence (on E4) and finish. But as the feedback grows, D#4 is transformed first into a B4 and then up towards a G5—only to break off into a sudden rupture of dramatic silence, the last moments of the sound ragged, as though cut short. The final phrase of the chorus ("O'er the land of the free," bars 20–21) starts once more from a low B3, makes its way to B4, feeds back and bends dramatically downwards, before ending with the last two bars of anthem ("and the home of the brave")—the E4 on which it ends swallowed up by feedback and barely controlled noise. As if coming from some quite different musical context, a completely unexpected cadence is then heard (see example 2.1), using sounds with such a slow attack that they seem to specify an organ more than a guitar—a kind of "Amen" tagged onto the end of the anthem. A final cloud of feedback and guitar noise leads into the B♭/E tritone alternations (the same pitches that disrupted the anthem melody at 1:44; see example 2.1) that herald the start of "Purple Haze." Although literally completed, the anthem is left utterly "undone"—functioning as a kind of extended recitative introduction into Hendrix's own "anthem."

Specifications

What do the sounds of this performance specify? The preceding analytical description has already suggested some ways in which the sounds specify a number of different varieties of disruption or instability—and instability indeed seems to be an overriding feature of the performance. What is striking, however, is that this is specified in a number of different domains—from the sonic to the ideological—which might usually be regarded as operating at rather different levels. As illustrated in a schematic fashion in figure 2.1, three kinds of instability, ranging from cultural practices and the individual identity of the performer to the perceived sources of the sound itself, are specified in this performance, and do not differ in their immediacy—even if they require different durations of material to become audible. It may be *quicker* to hear that the opening sounds specify the pitch event G5 than to hear that they specify Hendrix, or the American national anthem, but this is not because the identity of Hendrix or "The Star Spangled Banner" are more abstract than the pitch: they are simply specified over a greater duration of perceptual information.

Figure 2.1 illustrates a small subset of the potentially large number of domains (or "sources") that the sounds of this performance specify. Starting with the category of "cultural practices," the pitch and rhythm pattern of the opening notes of the performance specify the American national anthem, which itself is a part of the cultural construct "Nationalism"—and these opening notes (as well as those that follow) thus also specify that cultural category. In opposition to that, and disrupting and destabilizing it, is the abundant perceptual information (the guitar, pitch bending, feedback, etc.) that specifies rock music and the youth culture of which it is a part—and just as the anthem is part of the larger construct "Nationalism," so too rock music is part of youth culture and its attitude of dissent and resistance. Nationalism and its counterculture are simultaneously and antagonistically specified in the sounds of the performance. The characteristic expressive nuances, and gui-

Factors that specify unstable or mutually antagonistic cultural practices:
• Pitch & rhythm pattern => American National Anthem (Nationalism)
• Instrumentation => Rock, Youth Culture (Counterculture)
• Expressive nuances/guitar timbre => Jimi Hendrix (Black American rock music)

Factors that specify instability in the musical material
• Pitch Bend => Breakdown of the discrete/continuous distinction in pitch.
• Rock treatment of Anthem (e.g. trilling thirds, pitch bend) => Breakdown of genre identity
• Disruption and transformation of Anthem (e.g. into arpeggiation/"Taps") => Breakdown of "Anthem as object"

Factors that specify instability in the sound
• Distortion (high electrical gain) => Instability of pitch & timbre
• Fluctuation of loudness/timbre (Leslie speakers) => Spatial instability
• Feedback (gain) => Instability of instrument and mode of production.

Figure 2.1   Schematic representation of three domains of perceptual meaning in Jimi Hendrix's performance of "The Star Spangled Banner."

tar sound, of the performance also specify the identity of Jimi Hendrix as performer, whose status as a black American rock musician and "countercultural hero" aligns him with an antagonism towards conventional American nationalism.

The next domain in figure 2.1 concerns the instability of musical material. As alluded to earlier, the juxtaposition of pitch bends and glides with discrete pitches strikes at a fundamental distinction (continuous vs. discrete) in the musical material itself, just as the interpenetration of the musical devices of rock music with those of the anthem, and the fragmentation or transformation of the anthem, strike at the musical identity of "The Star Spangled Banner." This disruption or destruction of the anthem's identity is as much concerned with a cultural taboo as with a musical object—and could equally feature in the first category of figure 2.1. As already observed, national anthems are conventionally regarded as important emblems of nationhood, to be treated with very much the same respect as national flags. The treatment of the anthem in this performance breaks that taboo in much the same way as do burning, defacing, or irreverently juxtaposing the national flag.

Lastly, in figure 2.1 there is sonic instability, most of the features of which I have already described in the preceding account of the performance. There are the timbral and pitch instabilities that are directly specified in distorted and "noisy" guitar sounds, the spatial instability that comes from the constantly changing dynamic and spectral characteristics of sound projected through rotating Leslie speakers, and the instability or uncertainty of instrument and "mode of activation" (plucked vs. induced by sympathetic resonance) that the use of feedback induces. Each of these effects is specified in properties of the sound itself—and at the heart of it all is ambivalence and uncertainty: what pitch does an inharmonic complex specify? Where is a constantly changing sound located in space? What kind of instrument is this that both "sings" and is plucked?

In summary, as the figure and associated discussion are intended to show, the perceptual meaning and critical value of this performance are specified in a number of domains simultaneously. Culture and ideology are just as material (in the concreteness of the practices that embody them) as are the instrument and human body that generate this performance, and, as perceptual sources, they are just as much a part of the total environment. These are not "interpretations" drawn out of thin air and arbitrarily imposed on the music; they are specifications of the material relative to listeners enculturated in a particular context.

3 ⁓

Music, Motion, and Subjectivity

Having made the case for an ecological approach to music perception, and having shown how it might be applied to a specific musical example, in this and the next chapter I explore two different aspects of the way in which listeners engage with music. Chapter 4 looks at the way in which musical materials help to determine the "subject-position," or listening perspective, that a listener adopts; while this chapter deals with a more bodily and somatic aspect of that engagement, through the sense of motion[1] that a listener may perceive in music.

Although a listener's relationship with music is primarily an auditory one, it is far from solely auditory. The interdependence between perception and action that is emphasized in ecological theory suggests that every perceptual experience will bear the trace of an action component. In the case of music, these traces are not hard to find—they are displayed overtly in the foot-tapping, head-nodding and body-swaying that are commonly observed in even the constrained circumstances of the Western art music tradition. In many other traditions, the relationship is much more dramatically obvious. There has been increasing interest in the relationship between music and the body (e.g. Lidov 1987; Shove and Repp 1995; Clarke and Davidson 1998), and recent discussions in neuroscience of so-called mirror neurons (nerve cells in the motor area of the brain that show imitative activity when a perceiver observes another individual performing specific actions) suggest the possibility of a very deep-seated perception-action coupling. Ramachandran (2000) has suggested that mirror neurons may be the "single most important 'unreported' . . . story of the decade," and that their generalized mimetic function may hold the key to understanding the evolutionary development of distinctively human culture—including language, art, and music. For at least three reasons, therefore, there is a close relationship between sound (musical and everyday) and motion:[2] (1) sound is a direct consequence and indicator of motion, as in the clatter of stones down a hillside, the distinctive pitch and dynamic profile of a passing motorbike, or the creak of a branch swaying in the wind; (2) the relationship between auditory perception and human action is encapsulated in the functions of mirror neurons or the more general sensorimotor contingencies discussed by Noë and others (e.g., Hurley and Noë 2003; Noë 2003); (3) the production of musical sound requires and inevitably involves movement, from the relatively discreet movements of the vocal tract in singing, to the more manifest movements of hand-clapping and instrumental performance.

There is a long history of writing on the relationship between music and motion, dating back to classical Greek writings on music (see Barker 1989). My approach in this chapter is to argue that the sense of motion when listening to music is an inevitable consequence of the event-detecting nature of the human auditory system; that there are some interesting questions about *what* listeners perceive as being in motion; and that the varieties of motion specified in musical sound together constitute a crucial component of listeners' perceptions of meaning in music. In short, the relationship between music and motion is a fundamental aspect of music's impact and meaning; is significantly, but not only, concerned with the perception of self-motion; and should be regarded as a truly perceptual relationship—even though the perceived motion may be illusory (in the sense of being attributed to virtual, rather than real, objects).

As an emblematic example, consider the first and second subjects of the first movement of Beethoven's Fifth Symphony (Op. 67). Virtually every program note, CD liner, or record sleeve comments on the contrast between the dramatic and explosive character of the first subject material and the lyrical and flowing character of the second. But what or who is being dramatic and explosive on the one hand and lyrical and flowing on the other? Do listeners subjectively identify with the music and hear *themselves* acting out explosive or flowing actions, or do they hear these sounds as specifying the actions of *other* agents or objects? If the latter, then are these actions the abstract and metaphorical movements of musical material, or the real movements made by the performing musicians, or the imagined movements of fictional characters?

Music and Motion

The sense of motion in music has been closely associated with rhythm and tempo (most of the conventional terminology for tempo is motion-based). At the start of his historical overview of rhythmic theory, Yeston (1976: 1) observes that "In the broadest sense, the theory of musical rhythm has always been concerned with the elucidation of musical motion—motion that is differentiated by the durational value, pitch, or intensity of sounds, but which, at the same time, presumably exhibits certain regularities."

But the term "musical motion" is a slippery one, since it skirts around the question of what is moving, and in what kind of "space." Yeston's own perspective lies firmly within a tradition of structuralist music theory—score-based and abstract. By contrast, Shove and Repp (1995), who provide an important survey of motion literature relating to musical performance, offer a very different perspective on music and motion, one that focuses on the actual movements of performing musicians as an important and curiously overlooked source of the sense of motion that listeners experience.

> Traditionally, to explain the source of musical motion, theorists, philosophers and psychologists alike have turned to musical structure, which by most accounts is abstract. This has led some to believe that the motion heard is virtual, illusory or abstract. . . . Hidden from this view is perhaps the most obvious source of musical movement: the human performer. Why have so many theorists failed to acknowledge that musical movement is, among other things, *human* movement? (Shove and Repp 1995: 58; emphasis in original)

Shove and Repp examine the ways in which the real (or imagined) motion of the performer may be specified in sound, and the ways in which the movements of both performers and listeners might be used to increase their aesthetic engagement with music. In doing so, they demonstrate that a number of German writers in the early part of the twentieth century (Sievers, Becking, Truslit; see Shove and Repp 1995) were particularly interested in the relationship between body movement, gesture, and performance. Each of these authors developed his own lexicon of movement types, the function of which was both analytical and practical: each lexicon was intended both to reveal, and make sense of, the inner dynamics of music, and in this way to help performers to find a fluent and expressive approach in performance. Becking, whose ideas were subsequently taken up and developed by Clynes (e.g. Clynes 1983), distinguished a number of types or styles of movement curve, and attributed these different styles of movement to the music of different groups of composers. Truslit (1938; see Repp 1993) had no interest in the composer specificity of musical motion, but was more concerned with the relationship between the acoustic surface of a musical performance and the underlying motion dynamics of the piece. He was interested therefore in the specifics of individual pieces and in discovering particular movement patterns that would help listeners and performers to understand and project the music

in the most effective manner. One feature of his theory is the proposal that performers' larger (more global) and smaller (more local)
movements (and the mirroring physical responses of listeners, such
as foot-tapping, head-nodding, swaying, and so on) reflect the
organization of the human motor system into two divisions—one
controlling whole body movement, and the other more peripheral
limb movements. The former (the ventromedial system) is closely
associated with the vestibular apparatus in the inner ear, which is
responsible for our sense of balance and motion, thus suggesting a
possible direct physiological link between the perception of sound
and the sense of bodily motion.

Although Shove and Repp briefly consider the wider specification of motion in music (i.e., motion that is not necessarily
attributable to the performer, but to some other agent, such as the
listener's own motion, or the motion of some virtual agent) this is
not the main focus of their review. Todd, however, has paid rather
more attention to listening and the sense of motion that it can
induce. In a paper concerned with the relationship between tempo
and dynamics in performance, he concludes with the proposal that
expression in performance has its origins in simple motor actions,
that the performance and perception of tempo and dynamics is
based on an internal sense of motion, and that "expressive sounds
can induce a percept of self-motion in the listener"(Todd 1992:
3549). The basis for this, he speculates, may lie in the physiology
of the vestibular apparatus in the inner ear, and in the possibility that sound directly activates that part of it (the saccule) that
is responsible for a person's sense of self-motion. In a subsequent
paper, he notes the need to be cautious about the relationship
between musical expression and physical motion, distinguishing
between "purely metaphorical notions of musical motions and any
more psychologically concrete phenomena that correspond to the
metaphorical" (Todd 1995: 1946). More recently (Todd 1999), he
has argued strongly for a vestibular component within the sense
of musical motion, complemented by a sensorimotor element.
Rather like Truslit, he has suggested that these two systems possibly

map onto the distinction between smaller-scale gestural motion (movements of the limbs) and larger-scale whole body movement, respectively.

Empirical evidence for the perception of motion in rhythm is provided by Gabrielsson (1973), who asked listeners to rate a collection of simple rhythmic figures using a large number of descriptors. The descriptors attributed to the rhythms clustered together according to three main principles: those concerned with structure, which related to the complexity of the rhythmic patterns and their meter (triple or duple); those relating to the emotional quality of the rhythms; and, finally, descriptors relating to the motion character of the rhythms, involving words such as "running," "limping," "flowing," "crawling," and so on. Given music's long history of association with a variety of physical activities (dancing, singing while working, marching, performing ceremonial actions), this finding might not seem too surprising, but the spontaneous emergence of this factor in Gabrielsson's research comes from a laboratory study in which very simple rhythms were played on a single drum. The implication is that this motion character is a pervasive and deep-seated component of listeners' responses to even quite simplified musical materials.

The Metaphor of Motion

In their different ways, Shove and Repp, Todd, and Gabrielsson all treat motion in music as a more or less concrete perceptual phenomenon. But it has been widely claimed that the sense of motion in music—like the sense of space in music—is essentially metaphorical.[3] There is, after all, no real space that musical materials inhabit (so the argument goes), and musical elements (pitches, rhythms, textures, etc.) have no concrete material existence. Therefore, since motion is a property of objects in space, the whole idea of musical motion—if taken literally—is a nonstarter. In *The Aesthetics of Music*, Scruton (1997) gives serious attention to a consideration of music's motion character from precisely the perspective of its fundamentally metaphorical character. The starting point for Scruton's argument is the distinction between sound and tone, which he identifies in three specific attributes: the distinction between what he calls the "acoustical experience of sounds" and the "musical experience of tones"; the distinction between the "real causality" of sounds and the "virtual causality" that relates tones to one another in music; and finally the distinction between the sequence of sounds and the movement of tones that listeners hear (Scruton 1997: 19). As these distinctions make clear, Scruton argues strenuously for a fundamental distinction between the sounds of the "everyday" world and the tones of music. This crucially places listeners' motion experiences in a realm that is quite separate from their auditory experiences of the motion character of everyday objects in the "real" world—the sound of footsteps approaching, of cars passing, of balls bouncing, of bottles breaking, of water gushing, and so on. Scruton nonetheless places the sense of motion at the center of musical experience: "Whenever we hear music, we hear movement," he writes (55), and ". . . we *must* hear the movement in music, if we are to hear it as music" (52; emphasis in original).

His explanation for this sense of movement in music, relating as it does to an acousmatic space divorced from the real spaces of the world, is that it depends on a deep-seated metaphor:

> [The] idea of musical movement is an irreducible metaphor, which can be explained only through our response to music. It is associated with other metaphors—and in particular with the metaphor of life. In hearing the movement in music we are hearing life—life conscious of itself. . . . (353)

Elsewhere he suggests that we "think of music as spread out in acousmatic space, where a new kind of individual is born and lives out its life: an individual whose character is constantly changing in response to the musical surroundings" (72). Scruton's approach is a consequence of the fundamental claim that musical events are "secondary qualities"—not tied to, or a part of, the physical circumstances of the real world but separated from them, and capable of behaving in ways that are not constrained by the real world. His notion of movement and gesture is abstract and idealized because the entities that move (notes in a melody, or a chord within a sequence) have no reality as physical objects. Musical motion and space are metaphorical because the properties of *real* space and motion have been transferred across to another domain where they have no literal application. Despite referring approvingly to the work of Lakoff and Johnson, who argue that metaphor occupies a central position in human cognition (Lakoff and Johnson 1980; 1999), Scruton asserts that "all metaphors are false"(1997: 91). By drawing a clear line between the tangible and practical world of sound, and the abstract and incorporeal domain of tone, Scruton places music firmly in a metaphysical realm and aligns himself definitively with the aesthetic tradition of music's autonomy.

But why insist upon the separation between sound and tone? The sounds of music can and obviously do specify objects and events in the world (instruments and the people who play them), and kinds of action (bowing, blowing, plucking, striking), even when the precise nature of those actions is unclear or uncertain (a person may hear striking without knowing exactly what is being struck). In this most obvious sense the sounds of music *are* the sounds of the everyday world. A listening strategy that was concerned solely with the objects and actions of instrumental performance might be rather limited (although the importance of music's instrumental character has until quite recently been seriously undervalued by both musicology and the psychology of music), but a range of other possibilities is opened up by considering the way in which musical sounds may specify the objects and events of a *virtual* environment. In visual art, an important part of the perceptual experience of looking at a painting (representational or abstract), is to see the forms and colors of the painted surface as specifying virtual objects in a virtual space with properties that are reminiscent of everyday objects and spaces—or (as in of some of M. C. Escher's drawings, for example) scenes that fascinate their viewers by defying or playing with the normal rules of space. The same principle applies to hearing: sounds can specify a virtual domain that both abides by, and stretches or defies, the normal laws of physics.[4]

Gjerdingen (1999) gives an account of what he calls apparent motion in music that takes as its starting point the analogy between apparent motion in vision and in music. A well-known illusion in vision, known as the "phi effect" (Kolers 1972), can be created by placing two lights a small distance apart, switching on and off in alternation with one another. When spaced at an appropriate distance, and flashing within the appropriate range of rates, people report a compelling sense of movement from one light to the other.[5] Similarly, two notes spaced an appropriate interval apart, and alternating at an appropriate rate, will give rise to an "apparent movement" between the notes. However, Gjerdingen asserts that

> if musicians—and listeners in general—concur in sensing motion in music, there is little agreement about the *nature* of the motion. . . . In viewing a classic visual demonstration of apparent motion, one can easily imagine an intermittently flashing light source that moves in normal three-dimensional space. In hearing the subject of a Bach fugue, however, it is not at all clear what is moving or where that motion takes place. (Gjerdingen 1999: 142; emphasis added)

His own approach presents apparent motion as motion in a unidimensional pitch space (simply lower to higher) over time. Implemented as a neural network, his model provides a graphic output that seems to capture many of the apparent motion effects that listeners hear in the context of phenomena such as the pitch streaming of interleaved parts, scalar and arpeggiated pitch patterns, trills, and the separation or integration of parallel parts. Persuasive though the demonstrations are, they leave a basic question unaddressed—the issue which Gjerdingen himself identifies in the extract above: *what* is moving and in what kind of space does this motion occur?

The Perceptual Reality of Motion in Music

Recall the unlabeled CD discussed at the beginning of the introduction, with its recording of someone eating crisps from a packet. The sounds of that recording specify, among other things, the crackly movements of the crisp packet, the mouth movements of the person eating, and so on. When I hear these events over a pair of loudspeakers or headphones, I am under no illusion that the packet of crisps or the person eating them are concealed somewhere within the loudspeakers or the headphones, just as when I watch a newsreader on television I do not mistakenly believe that she is actually in the set. But neither do I see the newsreader's movements, or hear the crackling and crunching of the crisps, as metaphorical events. I perceive them as perfectly real, but I also perceive that these events are broadcast or recorded, and that the actual events are not happening here and now. In the same way, the study by Warren and Verbrugge (1984) of the perception of bouncing and breaking, referred to in chapter 1, showed that listeners could reliably distinguish between the two kinds of event on the basis of sound recordings of auditory sequences, or artificial simulations of those sequences that preserved the principal temporal properties of the originals. These recordings or simulations are not heard as specifying apparent, or metaphorical, events: they specify perceptually real events that happen not to be present.

A solution to this problem of the perceptual reality, but physical absence, of recorded events is provided by the idea of a "virtual source"—an idea developed by McAdams (1984); and it is with this idea that ecological theory provides an explanation of the perception of motion in music. McAdams coined the term "virtual source" by analogy with the term virtual image (or virtual object) in optics, where it refers to the objects and images seen in mirrors and pictures, and which occupy the virtual space behind the plane of the picture or mirror. In a similar manner, musical sounds may be organized in such a way that they specify a source that has no real, physical existence. Various tricks of orchestration are an obvious example, where the impression of a "virtual instrument" that has no empirical presence can be created through the fusion of sounds coming from various actual sources. Bregman (1990: 460), in an extensive discussion of auditory perception organized around the central idea of "auditory scene analysis," points out that "the virtual source in music plays the same perceptual role as our perception of a real source does in natural environments." The psychological processes involved in perceiving real and virtual sources are identical, just as the experiences themselves may be equally vivid and apparently veridical—but while one refers to real objects and events in the world, the other does not. "Experiences of real sources and of virtual sources . . . are different not in terms of their psychological properties, but in the reality of the things that they refer to in the real world. Real sources tell a true story; virtual sources are fictional" (Bregman 1990: 460).

In the case of a mirror, the virtual objects that can be seen in it have a lawful relationship with the real objects of which they are a reflection, move in a fashion that corresponds directly to the movements of their real counterparts (of which they are a reflection), and are described by an optics identical to that of the real world (though reversed). In a picture, film, or animation, the objects have qualities that may mimic those of the real world, and can do so very convincingly in the case of *trompe l'oeil* painting, or computer animation, but these qualities are achieved using quite different means. In a discussion of painting and drawing (Gibson 1966: 240), Gibson pointed out that Hans Holbein, in his portrait of Sir Thomas More, achieved the sense of folding and texture on More's velvet sleeve by using pigments of different hues, while the same visual effect on a real piece of velvet is produced by differential reflectance and shadow. Gibson noted the intriguing duality of a picture—the fact that the marked surface is both an object and also a medium by means of which a viewer may perceive other virtual objects:

A picture, photographic or chirographic, is always a treated surface, and it is always seen in a context of other nonpictorial surfaces. Along with the invariants for the depicted layout of surfaces, there are invariants for the surface as such. It is a plaster wall, or a sheet of canvas, a panel, a screen, or a piece of paper. . . . The information displayed is dual. The picture is both a scene and a surface, and the scene is paradoxically *behind* the surface. (Gibson 1979: 281; emphasis in original)

The comparison with painting is instructive because it suggests a way of understanding both what is perceived as moving in music, and how the effect is produced. Just as spatial patterns of pigment in a painting can create a perceptual effect analogous to that produced by reflection, texture, and shadow in the real world, so music may create perceptual effects with temporal patterns of discrete pitches that reproduce, or approximate, those that we experience with the continuous acoustical transformations that are characteristic of real-world events.

Motion, Gesture, Meaning

While it seems obvious that visual information can specify motion, there is more resistance to the idea that the same might be true of sound. Certain kinds of acoustical invariants are readily accepted as specifying motion (e.g. a continuous change in left ear/right ear intensity balance or phase relation; or the pitch shift of the Doppler effect) since these directly specify real movement in real space. The experience of vivid sound tracks or demonstration sequences in surround-sound music systems or Dolby Digital cinemas are an indicator of how powerful this effect can be even when artificially generated. But a much more general possibility is that changing patterns of attack point, timbre, dynamic, and pitch have the capacity to specify motion in a virtual space—in the same way that the continuous spatial displacements of visual edges, points of light, swirls and textures in computer animation do.

> Transformations in loudness, timbre, and other acoustic properties may allow the listener to conclude that the maker of a sound is drawing nearer, becoming weaker or more aggressive, or changing in other ways. (Bregman 1990: 469)

Just as the success of animation depends on the propensity of the visual system to detect movement in even quite poor approximations to the visual arrays that specify real movement, so too the perception of motion and gesture in music relies on the detection of motional and gestural invariants in sound sequences which may, in objective terms, be quite poor approximations to their real-world counterparts. An orchestral performance of the opening motif of Beethoven's Fifth Symphony may have relatively little literal acoustical similarity to the sound of a hand knocking at a door, but it is sufficient for generations of listeners (guided by suggestive program notes and CD liners) to hear the "knocking of fate."

The basic principle can be stated simply enough: since sounds in the everyday world specify (among other things) the motional characteristics of their sources, it is inevitable that musical sounds will also specify movements and gestures—both the real movements and gestures involved in actually producing music (as discussed by Shove and Repp 1995, for example) and also the fictional movements and gestures of the virtual environment which they conjure up. As Windsor (1995; 2000) has discussed, acousmatic music[6] provides a context in which this is particularly striking, since the absence of any visual anchor allows free play within the virtual spaces that the music specifies. In certain respects, this is not a new idea at all: Langer (1942) wrote of the connection between musical meaning and music's capacity to convey movement and gesture, but the difference here is my claim that this relationship is truly perceptual rather than metaphorical, symbolic, or analogical. For the obvious adaptive reasons of getting around and surviving in an unpredictable environment, the auditory system is highly attuned to the motion-specifying properties of sounds, and since the variety of ways in which animate and inanimate objects may move is unlimited, every musical sound has the capacity to specify *some* kind of motion (or its opposite—stasis[7]).

Sounds specify motion by means of change[8] (discrete and continuous changes of pitch, timbre, and loudness over time); the crucial question is *what* a listener hears as being in motion. Todd has proposed that the perception of motion in music is a sense of *self*-motion, as a necessary consequence of the vestibular explanation that he proposes. If musical sound directly stimulates the vestibular apparatus, the group of organs in the inner ear responsible for monitoring a person's own balance and movement, then this will induce a sense of self-motion (Todd 1999). But a perceptual approach allows for the experience of either self-motion or the motion of other objects. The relativity of motion ("am I moving relative to the surroundings, or are the surroundings moving relative to me?") means that there is always potentially an uncertainty: when you look out of the window of a stationary train and see movement in relation to another train, the well-known perceptual jolt, as the apparent self-motion is suddenly revealed to be actual movement of the other train, is an illustration of this relativity. In a similar way, sound specifies motion but on its own cannot unambiguously specify the relativities of that motion: in terms of pitch shift, the Doppler effect, for example, is identical whether caused by a sound-emitting object approaching and passing a stationary observer, or a moving observer passing a stationary sound-emitting object. There is little empirical evidence about the extent to which listeners perceive musical motion as self-motion or as the movement of other objects, but some of the language that people use in relation to their musical experiences is indicative of self-motion: "moved," "swept away," "transported," "blown away" are just a few of the terms people use to describe intense musical experiences. In part this may be attributed to a simple principle of ecological acoustics: if all the separate sources (real or virtual) that are specified in a piece of music are heard to move together in a correlated fashion, this specifies a listener moving in relation to a collection of stationary sound sources (i.e. self-motion). If, however, the various sound sources all move relative to one another, and in relation to the listener, this specifies the movements of external objects in relation to one another. In very simple terms this suggests, for instance, that music with complex polyphonic properties is likely to be heard in the latter category—as the movement of external objects/agents in relation to one another and the listener; while monodic or homophonic music may more easily specify self-motion—movement of the listener in relation to the environment.

Three Musical Examples

Having considered the perceptual principles that may explain how music specifies motion, this section considers the particular musical features that specify motion in three rather different musical examples. The first example focuses on the pair of dramatic orchestral crescendos on a single pitch (B) that occurs in the interlude between scenes 2 and 3 of the third act of Alban Berg's opera *Wozzeck* (see example 3.1). The motion that is specified by these sounds is paradoxical. On the one hand the complete absence of pitch change specifies stasis, while on the other the continuous change in both timbre (in the first of the two crescendos) and dynamic (in both of them) specifies continuous and unidirectional motion. The net result is, perhaps, a sense of highly focused and unswerving approach—the auditory equivalent of what Gibson called "looming" or "time-to-contact." Gibson writes of the visual information that specifies the approach to, or approach of, an object as follows:

> Approach to a solid surface is specified by a centrifugal flow of the texture of the optic array. Approach to an object is specified by a magnification of the closed contour in the array corresponding to the edges of the object. A *uniform*

rate of approach is accompanied by an *accelerated* rate of
magnification. . . . The magnification reaches an explosive
rate in the last moments before contact. This accelerated
expansion . . . specifies imminent collision. (Gibson 1958
cited in Gibson 1979: 231; emphasis in original)

This description of the visual-information specifying approach
closely parallels the sounds of these two orchestral crescendos,
if one makes appropriate sensory substitutions: continuous
dynamic increase substitutes for flow of optical texture, and the
pitch stasis provides the centrifugal quality. (Imagine how different the effect of the example would be if the music were to
trace some kind of continuous or stepwise pitch trajectory at the
same time as the crescendo.) The "explosive rate" of magnification mentioned by Gibson, and the imminent collision that it
specifies, is an aspect of the *Wozzeck* example that is largely in the
hands of the conductor who controls by exactly how much, and
at what rate, Berg's dynamic markings should be realized. Karl
Böhm's 1965 recording of the opera,[9] however, does seem to reach
this "explosive rate" of intensity increase, and thus the sense of
imminent impact.

The two crescendos differ in a number of respects and give
rise to different motion effects as a result. The first crescendo is
achieved not only by continuous increases of dynamic within each
of the instruments or instrumental groups of the orchestra, but
also by a complex pattern of successive instrumental entries, so that
both the timbre and the texture of the orchestral sound change continuously as the dynamic increases. Arguably, this results in a less
focused and static "looming" quality than is achieved by the second
crescendo, which consists simply of a huge crescendo on an orchestral *tutti*. A second difference concerns the respective endpoints or
"contact moments" of the two crescendos. The first, after a build
up on unison B, ends with a six-note orchestral chord, which is
played as a rhythmic unison on a downbeat, and coincides with the
first note of the distinctive rhythmic figure played solo and triple

Example 3.1   The interlude between scenes 2 and 3 of Act III
of Alban Berg's opera *Wozzeck*.

forte by the bass drum (see example 3.1). The orchestral downbeat has the attack and unanimity of a physical impact, and the sense of motion that the first crescendo conveys is therefore of approach, followed by collision—out of which the bass drum appears with the suddenness of an explosive rupture. The second crescendo, by contrast, is an orchestral unison throughout and consists solely of a dynamic crescendo which ends *not* with a downbeat—indeed without any final "event" at all—but with the equivalent of a cinematic cut straight into the next scene of the opera. (Berg's instruction in the score is that the instruments should be quickly damped, to coincide with the curtain being rapidly raised on the next scene.) It is as if the imminent collision never materializes, and the listener (or the music?) is shot out into a new and completely unexpected space—as if passing through an invisible barrier at the moment when collision seemed inevitable. Using the similarity with optical flow, texture gradients, coordinated versus independent component behavior, and so on (the basis for which is already established within auditory scene analysis research[10]), it would be relatively straightforward to establish empirically what the musical/acoustical conditions are that specify collision, rupture, emergence, unidirectional movement, or movement with frequent directional change, and so on. It simply has not yet been done.

My second example comes from pop music—a short section from the track "Build It Up, Tear It Down" (from the CD *You've Come a Long Way, Baby*) by the British musician Fatboy Slim (Fatboy Slim 1998). The track, which is representative of techniques used in a considerable amount of recent dance music, starts with drum kit and other percussion sounds presented in a relatively dry (nonreverberant) acoustic, soon followed (at 0:15) by a male voice with rather more reverberation. This part of the track demonstrates no particularly unusual motion characteristics. However, at 0:28, the sound and texture abruptly change, a bass instrument of some kind replacing the previous percussion and vocals, playing the pitches B and E in alternation and heard as if through a low-pass filter (i.e. with most of the higher frequency components eliminated). Over the course of the next half-minute this sound continuously evolves as if the cut-off frequency of the low-pass filter is being progressively raised, the higher frequency components becoming more audible, and revealing the sounds of a drum kit (at about 0:40) and other instruments in the mix. As the filter cut-off rises, resulting in an increasingly bright and clear sound, the same male voice that was heard in the earlier part of the track is added to the mix (at 0:55), reaching a climax of volume, rhythmic density, and timbral brightness until it cuts into another louder and fuller texture (at 1:02) which is the principal material for the rest of the track.

The perceptual effect of the 34-second section described here (from 0:28 to 1:02) is of a continuous movement towards a sound source that is at first occluded but progressively reveals itself. It is not clear whether this specifies self-motion towards a stationary sound source, or a moving sound source that approaches a stationary listening point—but in either case there is a powerful sense of the source being at first concealed below some kind of acoustic horizon, above which it then progressively rises until it is fully revealed and directly in front of the listener by the time the texture changes at 1:02. The explanation for this strong sense of motion, and for the particular *style* of motion described here, comes straight from ecological principles: in everyday circumstances, the acoustic array from a sound source that is concealed in relation to a listener (behind a large object like a wall or a building, or below a horizon) will possess attenuated high frequencies due to simple masking principles. High frequencies are absorbed and dissipated in the environment more rapidly than low frequencies, leading to the characteristic "bass heavy" quality of amplified music heard at a distance (the "open air pop festival" sound). As the distance to the source decreases, or the degree of occlusion declines, the high frequencies increase in relative intensity, shifting the timbral balance towards increased brightness. It is for this reason that the continuous change in filtering on the Fatboy Slim track gives rise to a powerful sense of approach to (or approach by) a sound source—as does the *Wozzeck* example, but using a different acoustic parameter.

My final example comes from instrumental chamber music and addresses a somewhat different consideration: the role of motion in bringing about a sense of agency in music—of the listener being at times an "overhearer" of musical events, and at others a participant among them. The development section (bars 152–205) of Mozart's String Quintet in C Major (K. 515) features a dramatic shift from one instrumental texture to another and then back again at the start of the recapitulation (see example 3.2). The two textures specify very different kinds of perceived motion—differing not in speed, proximity, or trajectory, but in terms of multiplicity and unity. The opening texture of the development section (which is the same as the prevailing texture of much of the exposition) can be described as an interchange between the cello and first violin, with the second violin and two violas supplying a middle-register harmonic "filler" in continuous quavers. The cello and first violin play strongly contrasting material: clearly articulated and linearly rising arpeggios in the cello, more lyrical material in the violin. At bar 168, however, this texture changes abruptly into something far more abstractly contrapuntal, involving the ensemble as a whole, with four of the five instruments at any one time playing overlapping semibreves and minims in a sequence of suspensions and resolutions. One instrumental part always remains more mobile (a neighbor-note figure in quavers which threads its way from the cello up through the ensemble over the course of 15 bars), and from 185 this material becomes increasingly prominent. At 193 recognizable thematic material from the exposition returns, and the clearly differentiated instrumental texture from the start of the development is resumed at the point of recapitulation (at 205).

I hear this passage as embodying a distinct change in perceived motion (and then a change back again)—and one in which there is an associated transformation of the sense of agency. As revealed by the earlier discussion of the relativity of motion and self-motion, the perception of motion in music brings a listener into a very

Example 3.2   Bars 152–205 of the First Movement of Mozart's String
Quintet in C Major, K. 515.

Example 3.2 (*Continued*)

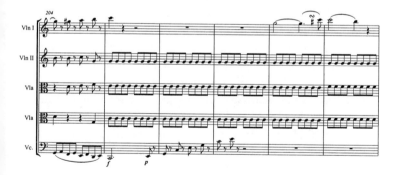

85

direct relationship with musical materials—as an agent among, or observing, other agents. I hear the opening of this Mozart development section more as an observer than a participant: the cello and violin parts specify very different kinds of motion (one assertive and energetic, the other receptive and accommodating), and for this reason, as well as for reasons of register and timbre, they specify distinct "agents" in motion relative to one another—two separate individuals. I *could* identify with either of them, or perhaps both in a kind of schizophrenic alternation—but actually I experience this as the actions of two separate agents of motion, with myself as onlooker (or "overhearer"). The inner parts have no particularly differentiated motion quality and provide a kind of environment—a ground against which the figures move. The textural change at 168 alters everything: the ground drops away as the inner instruments abruptly cease their regular quaver activity, and the separate parts merge into a single body with a complex movement, one with which I now identify, rather than simply overhear. There is a paradoxical quality to this single body in that its unified character (originating in its contrapuntal unity—a single source) coexists with an obvious sense of independent voices, emphasized by the overlapping, and frequently suspended, nature of the part writing. My own experience of the passage partially resolves the paradox by hearing it as the slow flexing, or intertwining, of the limbs of a single "body" with which I identify. This is, in other words, an experience of *self*-motion—while the earlier part of the development seemed more like the independent movements of others. As the texture again becomes more motivically differentiated (from about 184—see example 3.2), this sense of a single body starts to break up into distinct streams again, and by the start of the recapitulation the sense of separate agents, in relation to which I am an overhearer, is regained. The kinds of transformation described here, somewhat reminiscent of the kind of visual morphing that can be accomplished with computer animation, demonstrate how music has the capacity to call into question the rigid separation of subject and object and to play with states which do not wholly conform with either the one or the other. It shares this characteristic with other forms of "virtual reality": the player in a skateboarding computer game, for example, is commonly both subject (he or she is controlling the board, and the environment is frequently visualized from the perspective of the board) and object (the skateboard and rider will appear as an object in the scene) in a manner that the users of such videogames find intuitively convincing and unproblematic.

Another issue that these examples broach is the question of who or what is moving. As all three analyses illustrate, there is an ambiguity about the agency to which the movements described above should be attributed. In the case of *Wozzeck*, this is made more concrete and particular by the operatic context of the music and the drama of which it is a part. Does a listener hear him or herself as moving towards some collision, or as one of the characters of the opera moving towards some collision, or indeed as some other person or object in the drama? Given the dramatic context in which this brief musical interlude occurs (the main character, Wozzeck, has just murdered his lover, Marie, and will shortly drown himself), listeners may hear this as Wozzeck "rushing to meet his fate"[11] (or fate rushing to overtake him), or perhaps death rushing to meet Marie (heard now in immediate retrospect). But it is equally possible for a listener to hear this as self-motion, through an identification with one of the opera's characters—for me to hear myself as Wozzeck, for instance, hurtling towards disaster.

A reader might object that this discussion of the example from *Wozzeck* is unacceptably speculative, full of interpretive license, and basically out of step with an ecological approach: it seems to depend heavily on verbal and dramatic information to interpret the perceptual information (the sounds of the two orchestral crescendos)—rather than relying on specification by stimulus invariants. But this overlooks the fact that all of the elements mentioned (the drama, the characters, the sounds) *are* part of the available information for a viewer/listener. The considerable leeway that exists for different perceptions of this short musical extract is not a problem for an ecological approach: many much more mundane environmental circumstances can be perceived in more than one way, and aesthetic objects are particularly multivalent. Not only do the objects themselves often contain deliberately partial or conflicting perceptual information, with the consequence that they afford multiple possibilities; but the viewers/listeners who encounter them, even when drawn from notionally the same culture, may also differ markedly in their previous experience of these or similar events. Musical sounds are "underdetermined": on their own, they may often seem to specify many things—or maybe nothing in particular. But this can be strongly affected by the wider context in which they are heard: the regular quaver chords of the piano part in "Gute Nacht," the first song of Schubert's song cycle *Winterreise*, can be heard as specifying all kinds of motions and scenes, but a listener who knows the cycle's title, or has read the text of the first song in a program note, or even just seen a CD cover with an illustration of a wintry scene, is likely to hear this as footsteps in the snow; the information in the text or image serves to focus dramatically the potentially much wider range of scenes and actions that these sounds can specify. In this sense, as Nicholas Cook has argued (Cook 1998a; 2002), music almost always has a multimedia quality to it, and musical meaning is always the consequence of a context that is wider than the "sounds in themselves." The Fatboy Slim and Mozart examples leave open the interpretation of the scenes and motions that the sounds specify, as also does the *Wozzeck* example, even with its much more programmatic textual and dramatic context. But the general ecological principles proposed here constitute an explanatory framework that helps to understand not only the constraints that apply in this process, but also why there should be any perception of motion and agency in music in the first place.

Summary and Implications

This chapter has proposed that the sense of motion and gesture in music is a straightforwardly perceptual phenomenon, and that the process by which auditory information specifies motion in music is, broadly speaking, the same as the process by which motion is specified in everyday circumstances. Part of the motion that listeners perceive may be the real movements of the performers and instruments involved (Shove and Repp 1995), but an important component of the motion in music is neither real nor metaphorical, but fictional—in the same way that the scene portrayed in a picture may be fictional. The sense of motion or self-motion draws a listener into an engagement with the musical materials in a particularly dynamic manner (he or she seems to act among the materials), and in doing so constitutes a vital part of musical meaning. In particular, the sense of motion or self-motion raises intriguing questions of agency, as I have tried to show with the three musical examples presented here. Who or what is moving, with what style of movement, to what purpose (if any), and in what kind of virtual space? The theory proposed here has specific empirical implications that could be pursued—most obviously an investigation of the various kinds of perceptual information in music that specify motion and a consideration of whether they function in the same manner as perceptual information does for the motion of objects in everyday circumstances.

A number of authors have dealt with questions of subjectivity in music from various perspectives (e.g. Cumming 2000; DeNora 2000; Lidov 1987), and Watt and Ash (1998) have carried out empirical work demonstrating that listeners identify "person-like" qualities in music more readily than other types of attributes. Starting from a different perspective, but converging with the ideas presented here, Watt and Ash (1998: 49) conclude that "loosely speaking, music creates a virtual person." A common feature in all of this writing is the recognition that a listener's sense of meaning in music is powerfully bound up with his or her experience of being subjectively engaged (or alienated) by the music, and with the varieties of subjective states that music can afford. An important component of that subjective engagement with music is its corporeal, proprioceptive, and motional quality, which may on occasion provide listeners with experiences of "impossible worlds" that have some of the same attractions as do other forms of virtual reality.[12] Just as Cook (1998b) has argued that music is a means of gaining insight into other cultures and histories, and that we listen to music "not just for the good sounds, though there is that, but in order to gain some insight into those (sub)cultures" (129), so too music affords peculiarly direct insight into a limitless variety of subjective experiences of motion and embodiment—real and virtual.

4 ∾

Subject-Position in Music

When listeners perceive motion in music, they experience a particularly strong and quite physical identification with music. But this sense of subjective identification is not the only response to music that a listener may feel: at the other end of the spectrum there is the complete lack of engagement that may be experienced as indifference or alienation. As these extremes illustrate, and to reiterate a central principle of the ecological approach, perception must be understood as a relationship between environmentally available information and the capacities, sensitivities, and interests of a perceiver. A variety of different phenomena fall within the scope of this mutualism, but particularly important is the way in which the relationship between listener and music defines an aesthetic attitude. This is the primary focus of this chapter, and it represents a complementary perspective to that of chapter 3. While the sense of motion and agency both assume a close identification of a listener with the musical material, this chapter is concerned with the way in which music may afford a less immediate relationship—one in which a listener is both aware of what is going on in the music and what it might mean, and also has a sense of his or her own perspective on that meaning. This relationship is the focus of discussions of what has been called the "subject-position"—the way in which characteristics of the musical material shape the general character of a listener's response or engagement (involved, repelled, indifferent).

Subject-Position

The term "subject-position" has been widely used in cultural studies, and specifically in the context of film describes the way in which the construction of a film causes a viewer/listener to adopt a particular attitude to what she or he is witnessing. Johnston (1985: 245) characterizes the term as follows:

> We need to take into account a key conceptual distinction. On the one hand there is the empirical spectator whose interpretation of film will be determined by all manner of extraneous factors like personal biography, class origins, previous viewing experience, the variables of conditions of reception, etc. On the other hand the abstract notion of a 'subject-position', which could be defined as the way in which a film solicits, demands even, a certain closely circumscribed response from the reader by means of its own formal operations. . . . This distinction seems fruitful, inasmuch as it accepts that different individuals can interpret a text in different ways, while insisting that the text itself imposes definite limits on their room to manoeuvre. In other words, it promises a method which avoids the infinite pluralism which posits as many readings as there are readers, and an essentialism which asserts a single 'true' meaning.

The crucial distinction is between the empirical spectator and the subject-position: every spectator has a unique perspective on a film resulting from the individual's particular circumstances, experience, background, and aesthetic attitudes, as well as the specific viewing occasion. But the claim made by the idea of the "subject-position" is that there is a limit to this potentially infinite plurality, and that it is a limit that can be attributed to properties of the film itself—understood within a certain shared cultural context. The notion of a subject-position is an attempt to steer a middle course between the unconstrained relativism of reader-response theory (crudely put, the idea that perceivers construct their own utterly individual and unpredictable meanings from an aesthetic object) and the determinism (or essentialism as Johnston calls it) of rigid structuralism—the idea that meaning is entirely contained within the objective structures of the work itself.

In film, the manner in which formal devices may solicit or demand a certain kind of attitude to the events depicted results from the separation between the narrative content of the film and the manner in which viewers are allowed, or invited, to know about that narrative. As an example with connections to music, in Jane Campion's film *The Piano*, the viewer is encouraged to see the relationship of the central character (Ada) to her own impro-vised music as liberating, and to regard this music as a medium of unconstrained self expression—by contrast with the more prob-lematic relationship to her lover (Baines), which is mediated by the other (composed) music in the film. There are many ways in which the film achieves this, but a particular instance is a scene in which Ada returns with her daughter to a deserted beach, where they had previously landed with their belongings, to find and play her abandoned piano. The circling and flying movement of the camera around Ada at the piano, and the general sense of physical freedom and release of energy (reflected in her daughter's physi-cal play down at the water's edge) that this rapid, mobile but con-trolled camera-work produces, expresses a view of the music that she is playing (her music) as liberating and liberated. Expressed in simplified terms, the material under discussion here is "music" (of different kinds), and the subject-position that the film constructs (by virtue of the specific techniques of the film itself) is a portrayal of improvised music as a positive force in Ada's life, or as "unmediated self-expression" (see Purkis 1995).

This does not mean that every specific viewer will actually feel this way about improvised music in general, or the specific music in this film in particular. It is easy to imagine a spectator feeling irritated or affronted by what he or she might regard as an idealized and naive notion of music and its supposedly untainted capacity to express Ada's subjectivity. This might be the reaction of an "empirical subject" (to use Johnston's term), and is neither to be denied nor to be taken as a challenge to the notion of subject-position: indeed it is the separation between what *the film* seems to be doing (i.e. the subject-position that it adopts) and an individual's reaction to it that demonstrates that subject-position is distinct from "subjective reaction" (i.e. the response of an individual).

To apply this idea to music seems to require that some equivalent separation between "content" and "technique" be identified—just as the topic of "music" and the particular camerawork in the example from *The Piano* respectively occupy these two categories. In the case of instrumental music this raises issues to which I return at the end of the chapter. First, however, I will use the relationship between words and music in two pop songs to show how subject-position as a component of music's meaning is a direct consequence of the ecological perceptual principles presented in chapter 1. In each song, "Magdalena" by Frank Zappa and The Mothers of Invention, from the album *Just Another Band from LA*, and "Taut," by Polly Jean Harvey and John Parish from the album *Dance Hall at Louse Point,* I will show how features of the musical materials specify the subject-position of the song. In terms of textual content the two songs both deal with abusive relationships, but in contrasting narrative contexts and in very different musical styles. My approach, therefore, is to present an analysis of the material of the songs, before turning to a discussion of how ecological principles might account for this aspect of their meaning.

Magdalena

J*ust Another Band from LA* (CDZAP 25), originally released in
1972, contains live recordings from an appearance by Frank
Zappa and The Mothers of Invention in Los Angeles in 1971. The
album consists of a twenty-five minute caricature of a rock opera
("Billy the Mountain") and a suite of four songs, of which "Magdalena" is the third. The lyrics of "Magdalena" deal with an abusive
relationship between a father and his daughter, portrayed in a deliberately explicit and graphic manner. The song, which is a little over
six minutes long, has a fairly conventional verse/chorus structure,
but a tremendously extended coda takes up nearly half of the song's
duration and consists largely of a torrent of impassioned speech
over an increasingly frenzied two-chord vamp. The basic structure
of the song is shown in figure 4.1. In terms of "voice" structure,
the singer/speaker (Howard Kaylan) alternates between a narrating
role in the verses, and the first-person voice of the father in the choruses. He also takes the first-person voice of the father in the short
sung section labeled as the "Latin Interlude" (see figure 4.1), and
throughout the coda. Only once is the "voice" of Magdalena herself heard, when in verse five we briefly hear her, in Kaylan's theatrical falsetto, repel her father's advances. In terms of textual content,
the verses deal with the encounter between father and daughter,
while the choruses (all with identical lyrics) present a pathetic and
ludicrous appeal by the father to his daughter for her to trust him
and feel sympathy for him (see example 4.1).[1] The singing in the
Latin interlude (see below) is delivered entirely in a strained and
exaggerated falsetto voice—often an index of the absurd in Zappa's
music—and makes the transition from the first-person father's
voice of the chorus, which deals with less loaded verbal material,
to the verbally dense coda. This short falsetto interlude is also in
first-person voice, but now uses the more charged language that
appears in the verses combined with the pleading tone of the chorus. The coda itself, following what appears to be a conventionally

Time (Mins:Secs)	Material
0:00	Introduction (Instrumental)
0:07	Verse 1 (Sung)
0:22	Verse 2 (Instrumental + 'doo doo doo')
0:36	Verse 3 (Sung)
0:52	Chorus 1
1:42	Verse 4 (Instrumental + 'doo doo doo')
1:55	Verse 5 (Sung)
2:11	Chorus 2
3:00	Latin Interlude (Instrumental + sung + 'doo doo doo')
3:43	Coda (Singing turning to speech by 4.04)
6:24	End

Figure 4.1   Outline song structure for "Magdalena" by Frank Zappa
and the Mothers of Invention.

romantic start—but with a caustic twist ("Magdalena, Magdalena,
Magdalena, Magdalena, Daughter of the smog-filled winds of Los
Angeles")—rapidly becomes increasingly unhinged, and dissolves
into a barely controlled chaos.

Example 4.1   Chorus lyrics for "Magdalena" by Frank Zappa
and the Mothers of Invention.

My daughter dear,
Do not be concerned
When your Canadian
Daddy comes near
My daughter dear,
Do not be concerned
When your Canadian
Daddy comes near

I worked so hard,
Don't you understand,
Making maple syrup for the
Pancakes of our land
Do you have any idea
What that can do to a man
What that can do to a man
Do you have any idea
What that can do to a man
What that can do to a man

Like much of Zappa's music, the song is a collage of musical styles, each of which is executed with enormous skill and verve, but with a strong sense of irony—a feeling that nothing is intended seriously. The brief instrumental introduction, the majority of the verse and chorus material, and the "Latin interlude" are all jaunty and up-tempo in style (with a basic tempo of 120–130 bpm), with two exceptions: at the end of each verse on the word "Magdalena" and again towards the end of each chorus at the words, "Do you have any idea what that can do to a man?" the music suddenly switches to a rather overblown and mock-serious half tempo. The coda, which has something of the character of a sung and then spoken recitative, takes up this slow tempo (approximately 65 bpm), which it maintains until around 5:34, when a long accelerando starts (mirroring with the ever more hysterical lyrics), reaching a tempo of something like 220 bpm before dissolving into non-metrical chaos for the last few seconds of the track. The song is essentially in D major, but it exploits the cultural cliché of using fast tempi and the major mode when the lyrics are concerned with positive and active/projective emotions (the verses and the first two thirds of the chorus) and slow tempi and the relative minor for negative, passive, and unfulfilled emotions (Magdalena's name at the end of each verse, the last part of the chorus, ["Do you have any idea . . ."], and the whole of the coda—which consists of an unbroken alternation of root position B minor and first inversion F# minor chords).

This description gives some sense of the basic framework (textual, tempo, tonal) of the song, within which to consider the musical and ideological substance of the music, and the central question that the analyses in this chapter are intended to address: what subject-position does this music articulate, and how is that subject-position specified in terms of musical materials? The next step is to discuss some of the stylistic identities that this music employs, and to consider the interpretative stance towards them (and their associated lyrics) that is implied by the way in which they are presented. Fundamental to this approach is the proposal that it is the use of exaggeration and ridicule in the treatment of musical styles and the cultural values that they specify, together with features of the vocal delivery, that articulate the music's subject-position.

The instrumental introduction, with snare drum, guitars, keyboards and cymbals prominent in the mix, and all instruments playing in rhythmic unison, acts as a rather theatrical call to attention or fanfare and helps to establish melodrama as one of the primary "topics" of the track. This fanfare leads immediately into the first of three verses, and a rather wooden style of music that is somewhere between a marching band, and a country dance-band. The vocal line is a banally simple five-note ascending scalar melody that—as the lyrics list the father's "possessions," including his teenage daughter—gets stuck on a single note, taking the vocal phrase two beats beyond the point at which both the melody and harmony should have changed by the symmetrical conventions of this simple style. At the same time, the bright and breezy vocal manner with which Kaylan starts the verse shifts subtly towards a more menacing and tight sound[2] as he persists with his single note. As the first verse reaches its climax and conclusion, the vocal line breaks away from its single pitch up a five-note scale parallel to that of the first phrase before finishing in a lower register, with a breathy and melodramatic enunciation of the name "Magdalena."

The second verse keeps the same structure but is essentially instrumental: the vocal line is taken by guitar doubling the keyboard, and accompanied by falsetto "doo doo doo" harmony vocals singing in rhythmic unison with the line. In the context of such a vacuous melody, the overall effect is of a cheap and ludicrous banality, which again turns dramatic as the melodic climax of the verse is reached: the keyboard and guitar swoop down with a flourish before Kaylan finishes the otherwise wordless verse with the name "Magdalena" sung on a single note with the same mock seriousness as before. Verse three takes the narrative forward, following the pattern of the first verse, but gets even more stuck on a single pitch, with the consequence that the phrase structure extends even further (six beats) beyond its expected boundary. The lyrics are more sexually explicit, and the father's obsession comes across in the unvarying pitch of the delivery and the manner in which he "abuses" the phrase structure and meter of the song itself. The verse finishes as before with Magdalena's name treated to the same overblown vocal and instrumental devices.

The music of the verses, with its wooden and conventional character, tells us that "this is a story of everyday nice folk" at the same time as the lyrics make it clear that it is nothing of the sort—or rather that there is a corrupt and hidden "other world" concealed behind the well-ordered façade of conventional family life.[3] The unfolding narrative provides a glimpse in each verse of the father's abusive obsession, as the vocal line gets stuck on a single note, and the timbre of the narrating voice changes—a glimpse made more disturbing by the way it leads into the melodrama with which Magdalena's name—treated like a fetish object—is delivered.

The chorus that follows establishes a rather different style, reminiscent of the music of a Broadway show. It begins with harmony vocals, at first (from "My daughter" to "near"; see example 4.1 above) singing triplets against the continuing duple meter of the bass and other instruments, and giving the music a rather self-conscious quality as if trying to be clever. With the tempo halved, the instrumental sound is fuller and more relaxed than for the verses:

the bass plays a more varied line, the guitar and keyboards provide a rhythmically simple harmonic wash, and the kit playing gives the whole sound a loose mobility that comes from a more varied use of the snare drum and cymbals. Nonetheless, the deliberation of the vocal triplets gives this section a distinctly contrived quality, as do its stylistic associations: as the father tells his daughter not to "be concerned," the music suggests his deceit.

The second part of the chorus ("I worked" to "land"; see example 4.1) intensifies the rhythmic self-consciousness of the first part with a sequence of metrical transformations involving both simultaneous and successive triplet/duplet conflicts and transformations (first at "I worked so hard, don't you understand" and then at "making maple syrup for the pancakes of our land"; see example 4.1). The rather forced quality of these changes make this part of the chorus decidedly awkward and uncomfortable-sounding—as if the performers are the somewhat unwilling puppets of some other musical authority (a score or director). The jerky banality of the music that orchestrates the father's appeal to his daughter, with references to his hard-working life, portrays the man as a rather pitiful cog in the production of that most clichéd Canadian product—maple syrup. The man is as much a puppet of a faintly ludicrous machine as this awkward music is the "puppet" of Zappa's musical domination.

The final part of the chorus, released from the straitjacketed rhythms of the preceding section, breaks out into a grandiose E minor (the rest of the chorus revolves entirely around G and A major chords), with a vocal line swooping between normal and falsetto voice, heavy guitar chords, and much more ostentatious use of the drum kit. Particularly by contrast with the constricted quality of what has gone before, this is musical high drama, and it is used both to emphasize and ridicule the pitiful appeal by the father to his daughter's sympathy. With exaggerated stylistic contrast, the protagonist asks his daughter (and the overhearing listeners) to reflect, with melodramatic seriousness, on the question of what spending a life making maple syrup might have "done to a man." The sexual subtext—of what living in the same house as his teenage daughter might have "done to a man"—is the thinly concealed message.

At 3:00 the music moves into new territory: first a short section which starts instrumentally before adding vocals, the whole section in a kind of sanitized and caricatured Latin American dance style. This is "happy, good-time dance music," specified by the culturally stereotyped percussion and syncopated bass line, and nothing serious should be expected of it. The vocal is sung in an absurd falsetto, with exaggerated vibrato, and is framed within a symmetrical phrase structure and trite rhyming scheme, with other members of the band successively adding doo-wop backing vocals. Incongruously, the lyrical content consists of the father in first person pleading with Magdalena, and reassuring her that her mother won't find out. When the lyric comes to an end, the backing vocals are left manically repeating their "Dada dada dada, dup dup de yup" at breakneck speed on a tonally and timbrally unsettling bare B/F# fifth, and then, with an abrupt change to a more voluptuous sound, the backing vocals slide onto an F# minor chord, and the lengthy coda begins.

What do the materials of this "Latin interlude" add up to? Once again it is the exaggeratedly ironic contrast between words and music that is most striking: to the sound of up-tempo Latin dance music, with its conventional cultural specification of "carefree good times," the father sings of lust and deception expressed with provocative directness, but undermined by the absurdity of his vocal delivery and the banality of the musical materials. This situation is simultaneously dangerous, pathetic, and as laughable as the musical style is vacuous.

The rather more serious and sinister final twist introduced by the exposed backing vocals make a link to the music of the coda, which is suddenly completely different: relaxed, slow, lush, with a harmonic wash consisting of sustained backing vocals and keyboard sounds, and very light kit-playing consisting largely of cymbals with occasional little bits and pieces on the snare drum and tom-toms at the changes of harmony. The vocal line starts with an extravagant cliché—a descending arpeggio in F# minor over an octave and a half, that turns around at the bottom into an equally showy scalar ascent back to (and beyond) the starting point—and uses this to project the sardonic lines: "Magdalena, Magdalena, Magdalena, Magdalena, Daughter of the smog-filled winds of Los Angeles." Kaylan sings with a full, conventionally expressive, non-falsetto voice, but almost immediately, as the lyrics plunge into the father's lust-filled fantasy, the vocal sound becomes strained and pinched, with that same sense of barely controlled emotion and rising frenzy that is heard in milder form in the middle of each of the earlier verses. Within a further twenty seconds, the singing has degenerated into impassioned speech. The remainder of the coda is delivered in a style of rising dementia and uncontrolled emotions, to words that become increasingly deranged and abusive, laced with a catalogue of fetishized sexual and kitsch domestic images, Hollywood icons, and pure fantasy. The instrumental and vocal backing starts relatively detached, but from around 5:00 it becomes increasingly rhythmically forceful, and from 5:34, where the speech starts to become shouting, a gradual accelerando starts which continues over the next 45 seconds and reaches a tempo of something like 220 bpm before dissolving into uncontrolled and nonmetrical chaos for the final few seconds of the song.

The perspective taken by this long final section of the song is not hard to identify: on the one hand we are taken inside the mind of the father (since the whole of this part of the lyric is in the first person) and in some sense obliged to participate in his frenzy and mania, directly specified by the unbroken crescendo of rhythmic activity, dynamic level, rapidity of speech, and musical tempo. It is hard *not* to be drawn into this vortex of rising passion, not only because of the first-person voice of the text, but also because the music at the start of the coda is lush and beguiling by comparison with the faster and more awkward music that precedes it. By making less use of stylistic caricature, the music seems to address the listener in a more genuine and "authentic" manner. On the other hand the bluntness of the text, the garish mix of images (cultural, domestic, sexual), and the pathetic appeals of the father add up to an absurd collage that is clearly an object of irony and ridicule—as underlined by the background laughter of other members of the band and the audience at various points on the recording. The longer the music goes on, the more vacuous it seems (tonic/dominant alternation with doo wop vocals): combined with its melodramatic instrumentation and backing vocals, and the protracted accelerando, the effect is of a huge and mad fantasy with no substance.

This is why the song's subject-position is so uncomfortable: when listeners are invited to laugh at and ridicule the father's apparently cosy, small-minded and tacky "public" life with its neon Jesus pictures and maple syrup, are they also being asked to regard the dangerous and abusive relationship with his daughter as nothing more than a "ridiculous aberration"? And if they laugh (with surprise? embarrassment? discomfort? amusement?) at the father's actions and fantasies, do they collude in a smutty voyeurism? From the perspective of the daughter, this is no joke—as the menace in the father's voice during the coda suggests. The song withholds the easy comfort of a clear ideological perspective: it is neither a serious-minded indictment of abuse, nor is it simple indulgence in a smutty humor that colludes with the violence. It draws the listener into a world that is both laughable and shockingly unacceptable, and solicits both the collusion and the repugnance of the listener.

Taut

If "Magdalena" is an ambivalent and elusive case, the song "Taut," by Polly Jean Harvey and John Parish, is more directly confrontational. The song comes from the album *Dance Hall at Louse Point* (CID 8051/524 278-2) released in 1996, which consists of 12 songs co-written by Harvey and Parish (music by Parish, words by Harvey). "Taut" is just over three minutes long, and apart from the initial chorus with which it starts, is organized in

Time (Mins:Secs)	Material
0:00	Opening (Background sounds)
0:02	Chorus (Vocals alone)
0:27	Instrumental introduction
0:50	Verse 1
1:36	Chorus (Full)
2:00	Verse 2
2:45	Chorus (Full)
3:15	End

Figure 4.2   Outline song structure for "Taut" by Polly Jean Harvey
and John Parish.

a conventional verse/chorus alternation, as shown in figure 4.2.
The words, shown in example 4.2, are less graphic than Zappa's
for "Magdalena," but no less disturbing. Virtually all of the text
is in the first-person voice of the female "protagonist"—the only
exceptions being the two brief interjections by "Billy." Harvey's
vocal delivery is of three kinds: (i) the initial and final choruses
are in a thin, high vocal style, two double-tracked voices wavering
in pitch and clashing with one another; (ii) the middle chorus is
sung in full voice; (iii) the two verses are delivered in a rapid, close-
miked, semi-whispered speech.

Example 4.2   Lyrics for "Taut" by Polly Jean Harvey and John Parish.

Chorus 1

Jesus, save me
Jesus, save me

Verse 1

Can I tell you something?
Can I tell you a story?

It's about me an' Billy.
Cos . . . as I remember.
I remember it all started when he bought that car.
It was the first thing he ever owned apart from me.
An' the colour was red.
An' the colour was red an' he drove me . . .
he drove me out of my mind.
I am over it now.
It was Spring or Summer '65, I don't remember.
Steamin' an' sweatin' an' stickin' against the wheel.
An' I could see the tendons stand out in the back of his neck.
An' he used to make me pray.
Wearing a mask like a death's head.
When he put me there in the back seat.
Make me say, make me say:

Chorus 2

Jesus, save me
Jesus, save me

Verse 2

Inherited his father's hate is what he'd say
An' he'd cuss enough to strip the paint off heaven's gate
But somehow he could make joy come loose and truly alive . . .
An' I would do anything for him.
He just wasn't enough.
It was never enough.
He'd turn to me an' say, he'd, he'd say:
"Even the Son of God had to die, my darlin'"
An' he wanted everything, he wanted everything
He wanted the honey from the king.
Each new moon
He used to make me pray,
Hidden in the back seat there . . . Jesus,

He'd make me pray in there . . . where he wanted everything,
he wanted honey from the king,
"Say it:
Even the Son of God had to die, my darlin'. Hargh! Say it!"

Chorus 3

Jesus, save me
Jesus, save me

By contrast with "Magdalena," the music is stylistically homogeneous and free of the ironic play that is so audible in Zappa's
song. The track opens with about a second of rather hissy "silence"
before the initial chorus. The chorus itself (simply a descending E
major triad with an upper neighbor note on the initial B), recorded
at a low dynamic level and with a moderate amount of reverberation, sounds remote and otherworldly, an effect that is emphasized
by the hissy background "silence," and a sound of electrical hum
and crackle—as if a guitar with a poor electrical connection had
been left plugged in to an amplifier. This first chorus has the sound
of a distant location recording—two women singing somewhere
empty and deserted. Once the chorus has come to an end, and with
a moment more of the hissing silence that is the backdrop to the
opening of the song, two rhythm guitars start to play a short cycli-
cally repeating two-bar riff in a fast quaver rhythm (160 crotchet
bpm) based around two superimposed fifths (AEB) with a hard,
relentless sound (riff A, shown in example 4.3). The sound is distant and distorted—as if played at high gain through a distant or
low-powered amplifier—and has the same sense of remoteness as
the chorus.

After four repetitions of the two-bar unit, a chilling vocal creak
or shriek develops over four further repetitions of the guitar figure.
Neither the gender nor the location in the "sound stage" of this
voice are at first identifiable because of the constricted nature of the

Example 4.3   Initial rhythm guitar figure (riff A) for "Taut"
by Polly Jean Harvey and John Parish

sound itself, though the register suggests a woman's voice—which
the spoken delivery at the start of the verse confirms. The sound
conveys a strong sense of barely contained emotions, as though this
tight vocal sound might break out into something full-voiced, but
complicated by an uncertainty about what this might be (anger,
ecstasy, or terror).

The start of the first verse (at 0:50) is then marked by a number
of simultaneous changes:

- The rhythm guitars change to the riff shown in example
  4.4, both parts using quite a lot of pitch bend,[4] so that
  the combined sound is more dissonant—and often
  microtonally dissonant—than the opening figure (example 4.3), and less harmonically rooted.
- The drum kit enters, placed forward in the mix, and at a
  dominating dynamic level, playing the syncopated and
  discontinuous material shown in example 4.5.

Example 4.4   Combined rhythm guitar figure (riff B) at the start of the
first verse of "Taut" by Polly Jean Harvey and John Parish.

Example 4.5   Drum kit patterns for verses 1 and 2 of "Taut"
by Polly Jean Harvey and John Parish.

- Harvey's voice changes from its creak or shriek into an intensely whispered speaking voice, recorded close to the microphone with a lot of audible breath and at the very front of the sound stage.

The effect of these changes at the start of the verse is to disrupt and disturb the context established previously and to bring about a separation between two layers of sound—with the guitars relatively distant and somewhat remote, and the voice and drums much more forward and direct. If the music of the first 50 seconds establishes a sense of bleak and disengaged remoteness, the creak or shriek leading up to the first verse introduces directness, immediacy and a kind of pent-up urgency. Harvey's first words are "Can I tell you a story?," and the intensity of her whisper specifies the fear, secrecy, arousal or shame that she feels about that story. The kit-playing during the verse (example 4.5) is disruptively angular: intermittent and frequently on weak quaver beats, it acts like a commentary on Harvey's voice, filling in gaps between the lines of the lyric, sometimes jutting through them, using a mixture of isolated and more continuous drum, cymbal, and stick sounds with hardly a single repeated pattern and frequent gaps of silence. The 32-bar verse has a simple three-part structure: 8 bars of riff B (example 4.4); 16 bars of riff A (example 4.3); 8 bars of riff B—with an association between riff B and the kit, so that the kit plays at the beginning and end of the verse but is eerily silent in the middle. In the middle section of A material, as the kit drops out and Harvey tells us of Billy's car, the sound is briefly somewhat calmer and less chaotic, with more lyrical guitar fragments derived from riff A. But as the verse moves towards its climax and into the chorus, the kit re-enters—first just with stick sounds (at "sweatin' and stickin'") and then (when riff B returns) with explosive drum and cymbal shots.

The music in this first verse bristles with tension and the constant threat of breakdown. Only in the middle of the verse, as the more consonant riff A returns and the kit falls silent, is there some temporary and partial respite—the very section of the verse where Harvey tells us of Billy's car, and of this remembered time. Her whispered delivery is controlled—even calm—until she reaches the words "drove me out of my mind," where her voice is suddenly tighter and is followed by a slight gasp. The next line ("I am over it now") is delivered with the deliberation of a suppressed struggle, and as she tells us more of what she remembers, her delivery becomes rapid and broken up—as if once again losing that hard-won control.

The chorus into which this increasingly tense music erupts is an explosive release. Harvey sings with full voice in a thicker instrumental texture, a bass guitar (for the first time in the song) anchoring both the strong E major tonality, and the secure and regular meter. Gone is that sense of a bleak location recording that characterized the first chorus, with its colorless and washed-out sound now replaced by Harvey's strong and confident voice securely embedded within the instrumental texture.

Verse 2 is again 32 bars long, but divided even more simply into 16 bars of riff A and 16 bars of riff B. It is immediately more highly charged than the first verse, with Harvey's whispered delivery faster now, and almost incoherent at times. Between lines—even between words—there is a gasp or a sob, and halfway through the verse her whisper first rises to a squeak, and then drops to a growl between audibly clenched teeth. Even more disturbing is her deep-whispered delivery of Billy's ominous phrase "Even the son of God had to die, my darlin'," full of the conflicting emotions that accompany her memory—as she impersonates him. This is the voice of a person in an extreme state of some kind—a potent mixture of desire, fantasy, and terror. Silent throughout the first half of this second verse, the entry of the kit in the second half, with riff B, brings the same disruption and discontinuity as in the first verse, Harvey's voice reaching an emotional climax as she describes how "he wanted everything." The kit falls silent again before the end of the verse as Harvey's voice, suddenly restored to a menacing control and continuity, growl-whispers the final line—Billy's second threat that "Even the son of God had to die, my darlin'. Hargh! Say it!"

The final chorus brings the song full circle. By contrast with the vocal power of chorus 2, the thin and wavering double-tracked vocals from the opening of the song now reappear. The bass is there, as in chorus 2, but the kit stays silent until nearly halfway through the chorus, when it comes in with a more muted, distant, and reverberant sound than earlier. A partial fade-out to the thin texture of the start of the track has begun, leaving at the end an unresolved $^6_4$ chord on B with a seventh in the bass, and reverberating and receding drum and cymbal sounds. The song returns to the fragile world from which it began, with the sense that the protagonist is only "over it now" by virtue of a continuing effort of control and denial.

Subject-Position and Subject Matter

What subject-position does this collection of materials and procedures project? The song could hardly be further from the character of "Magdalena": no hint of irony, and not a trace of smutty voyeurism, collusion, or crude humor. This is uncompromising music whose position is clear—a serious confrontation with power, desire, and manipulation. The listener is made to face this frightening mixture, and experience its hold on a person.

What is it in the musical material that can account for the subject-position outlined here for "Taut" and, by contrast, for the rather more ambivalent subject-position claimed for "Magdalena"? Even before the first verse of "Taut" starts, in the first wordless 50 seconds of the song, a number of features of the sound specify a rather narrow set of conditions:

- The hissy silence at the start specifies a poor quality recording—not the sound of a modern studio.[5] This is the sound of either a historically distant, or an impoverished, reality.
- The absence of vibrato in the female voices singing in the opening chorus specifies a number of possibilities: naivety (a lack of conventional vocal training); a lack of engagement (going through the motions of singing—as if under duress); or "otherworldliness" (a lack of robust human physicality). Equally, the wavering intonation

specifies a lack of training or control; or a lack of concentration and commitment (singing unwillingly, or with distracted attention). A number of these same features (naivety, lack of robustness, lack of training or control) also give the sound its childlike quality.

- Until the start of chorus 2, there is no bass instrument and a predominance of high frequencies as a result. This spectral property specifies the rapid vibration of small or tightly stretched objects (the track title is "Taut")—in short, tension and a lack of "grounding."

- The timbre of Harvey's vocal creak or shriek in the run-up to the first verse directly specifies a tense and constricted vocal tract—symptomatic of a heightened and tense emotional state (ecstasy, fear, suspense).

- The guitar sound used throughout the song specifies a high level of physical energy (the strings are hit hard, the rhythm is fast) but an energy that is confined (the short riffs are static and encircled). This is high energy within confined limits, specifying tension or pressure.

- The hard and edgy guitar sound arguably specifies at least two partially overlapping cultural "sources": the music of The Velvet Underground, on the one hand, and punk on the other. Expressed in simplified terms, both these musical sources are connected with an alienated urban outlook, and as a result this sound now specifies that vision/ideology.

- The unpredictability, irregularity, and discontinuity of the kit playing specifies a particular type of control—a kind of manipulated unpredictability, but one which the listener is *subject to* rather than a part of.

- Almost everything about the sound of chorus 2 specifies a release from the tension and constriction of the first chorus and verse. The full and controlled sound of the voice specifies the confidence of "unharnessed" singing; the kit playing is regular, continuous, and reassuringly predictable; and the harmony is much more clearly defined and straightforward (unambiguous E major). This is part of the paradox and ambivalence of the song's subject matter: there is a kind exultation about the chorus, even though this is the frightening climax of a song that is concerned with domination and abuse.

- The final chorus is again ambivalent, but for different reasons. It has the tonal stability of the middle chorus, but two features call into question this "rootedness": the kit is absent, and as a result the texture sounds empty, devoid of the "power and exultation" of the previous chorus; and the strong and confident voice has been replaced by the weaker, wavering voices of the opening, which bring with them not only their earlier perceptual meanings, but now also the circularity and imprisonment of a return to the start of the song. The fading end of the song (a seventh chord, and reverberating kit) is the sound of something inconclusive: the song, the narrative, and the psychological drama are "unfinished business."

By contrast, "Magdalena" projects its shifting and ambiguous subject-position in a number of ways, including the following:

- The changes of "voice" (first person, third person) in the text.
- The singer's changing style of delivery (falsetto, head/chest voice, singing, semi-singing, speaking, ranting, and shouting).
- The frequent changes of musical style (dance band, show band, Latin band, "serious rock," 50s doo-wop).
- The use of caricature and excess: the falsetto voice (used extensively in the song) is an absurd voice "not to be taken seriously," because by convention (for instance in opera and pantomime) it frequently specifies a transparent

attempt by a man to fake either his sex (female) or his age (prepubertal). By contrast, the nonfalsetto voice in the coda is "genuine" in the sense of being truly impassioned, while the backing vocals are melodramatic and theatrical (falsetto, chorus-style) and serve to ridicule the father's increasingly deranged outpourings. Similarly, the extravagant vocal arpeggio at the start of the coda is a grand gesture that specifies a shallow and unconvincing rhetoric.

- Contrast and contradiction between the "tone" of the lyrics and the music: while in "Taut," intensity and fear are cospecified by the words and the music (with the result that the subject-position has a stark directness about it), in "Magdalena" the "tone" of the words often conflicts with that of the music. Examples are the "Latin interlude," where the happy banality of the music contrasts with the pleading and lustful words; and the verses where the ludicrous and wooden music (with the exception of the music that accompanies Magdalena's name) contrasts with words that continually veer off into obsession and fantasy. The result is the slippery and unsettling ambivalence that characterizes the song: two sources of information (words and music) specify incompatible psychological states.

This is far from an exhaustive account of the relationship between the sounds and what they specify in these two songs. But what these examples demonstrate is that the relationship between the characteristics of the sounds used and the subject-position specified can be traced in an explicit and principled manner, and that these relationships are part of an ecology that combines specification by social convention (e.g. the meaning of falsetto voice; the sound and ideology of punk or The Velvet Underground) and physical principles (e.g. the specification of a condition of the vocal tract by a creak/shriek; the specification of space or distance by reverberation).

The subject-position in "Magdalena" plays with the distancing quality of parody in relation to the song's subject matter, while "Taut" draws the listener in to a close identification with the singer and protagonist, through the song's confrontation with a potent mixture of infatuation and submission. Subject *matter* and subject-*position* interact in a compelling manner, and an important factor in this is that it is a singer-songwriter's material that the listener hears. As the singer and lyric-writer,[6] Polly Harvey inevitably takes on a close identity with the protagonist of "Taut." It is hard *not* to hear the song as a direct telling of something that happened to the singer herself when the first verse, after all, starts with the lines, "Can I tell you something? / Can I tell you a story? / It's about me an' Billy," delivered in a whisper with confessional directness. By contrast, after about six seconds of clichéd introductory music, the singer in "Magdalena" starts with the lines, "There was a man, a little ol' man / Who lived in Montreal." A more obviously narrative and distanced relationship between singer and subject matter could hardly be imagined. Neither song sticks to a single "voice," but because "Taut" is almost entirely first-person, its subject-position is heard as direct and "authentic": a fearful and disturbing identification, brought about by stark texture and timbre, unflinching rhythmic drive, and stylistic authenticity.[7] The subject matter is a story of the conflict between desire and fear: the wish to be "over it now" mixed with something unfulfilled ("it was never enough"). By contrast, the subject-position of "Magdalena" oscillates between mocking parody, brought about by the third-person voice, over-the-top vocal delivery, and stylistic caricature; and, in the coda, a more disturbing attempt to make the listener collude with the otherwise repugnant father, brought about by the first-person voice, the "sincerely" spoken delivery, and the more lush and less parodic musical style. The immediate subject matter is the repellent and slightly pathetic story of the father (for whom the listener is encouraged to have little sympathy—he is, for instance, described as "grubby" and "drooling") and his attempted abuse of his daughter—though the *real* subject matter is arguably the hypocrisy of middle-American culture, at which the listener is encouraged to laugh, or from which to recoil.

Subject-Position and Instrumental Music

How might the approach adopted here apply to other music— in particular instrumental music? When music has a text, the relationship between position and content can be identified in the way that it has been for the two songs: but when there is no text, what is subject matter? An answer might be to regard conventional musical materials, of the kind discussed by Tagg (2000), Tagg and Clarida (2003), or Agawu (1991) as subject matter (both in terms of musical materials and social content) and the particular treatment of the material as the specification of subject-position. When Zappa (or Stravinsky, for that matter) takes readymade material and "subjects" it to a transformation of one sort or another, or juxtaposes it with other material, the transformation specifies a position in relation to that subject matter. The separation between "material" and subject-position comes from an awareness of surplus, excess, or disjunction of one sort or another.

The guitar solo on "Dog Breath," the track that immediately follows "Magdalena" on *Just Another Band from LA*, provides an example. The solo is an example of Zappa's virtuoso guitar playing, but it incorporates the same ambivalence that is found in "Magdalena." It seems to demand both to be taken at face value (it is "heartfelt") and to be heard as ironic. The first half of the track employs falsetto vocals and melodramatic gestures for two verses and a chorus in very much the same way that they are used in "Magdalena," but at just over two minutes into the track the music breaks into a very clearly set-up guitar solo that lasts for nearly a minute and effectively completes the song. While the solo displays some of the hallmarks of Zappa's own idiosyncratic guitar style (a spiky and angular melodic shape and extensive use of the wah-

wah pedal) it also draws too heavily on the stereotypical conventions of rock guitar solos, and in too explicit a fashion, to be taken
entirely seriously. The chromatic descending bass line with static
harmony that provides the accompaniment is a clichéd archetype
over which innumerable long and frequently rambling guitar solos
were trotted out in the late 1960s and early 1970s. Similarly, the
use of register in the solo conforms to stereotype: a basically rising
trajectory across the solo as whole specifies the mounting excitement and increasing virtuosity that typifies a conventional rock
guitar solo, within which two discrete register changes (at 2:35 and
2:46) allow the guitar to jump into a higher, more cutting tessitura,
coupled with an increase in speed and virtuosity. This, too, is a
stock device in which a new level of intensity is reached by breaking
out of a register that had seemed to incarcerate the music—with all
the ideological associations of "individual freedom" and "heroic
struggle." This is a solo that, like "Magdalena," specifies a subject-
position that is characterized by a slippery ambivalence between
direct engagement and distanced parody.

Two further examples illustrate similar principles in rather different music. Stravinsky's neoclassical ballet music "Apollon Musagète," based on a French Baroque model, makes use of a whole
variety of stylistic "borrowings," with a greater or lesser degree of
self-consciousness and a correspondingly variable tone of (compositional) voice. In the penultimate movement of the work, however, there is a section that conveys a rather different subject-position from the rest of the work. The movement (entitled "Coda")
is firmly rooted in E major and comprises a series of sections with
a sequence of time signatures ($\frac{2}{4}$, $\frac{6}{8}$, $\frac{3}{4}$, $\frac{2}{2}$) and associated tempi that
create a sense of large-scale acceleration and mounting excitement.
From rehearsal number 71 to 89, a combination of syncopation
and irregular phrase lengths gives the music a slightly unpredictable and restless quality, which is then suddenly left behind at figure 89 (example 4.6). Here the music switches into an altogether
smoother and more predictable texture: a succession of 8-bar
phrases takes the music from figure 89 to one bar before 93, where

the whole section is repeated. As example 4.6 illustrates, the texture in this passage consists of three layers:

- A legato melody, doubled by the first violins and first cellos, marked *cantabile*, and organized into completely regular two bar units.
- A "walking bass" in the remaining cellos and basses, consisting of an uninterrupted succession of crotchets outlining tonal triads and the occasional seventh chord with a mixture of *marcato* and *pizzicato* articulation.
- A middle "filler" in the second violins and violas, consisting of a stereotyped "um-cha-cha" accompanying rhythm and basically triadic harmony.

This is a texture which is hardly distinguishable from that of a palm-court orchestra, with an easygoing tonal and metric quality that is consistent with this culturally conservative and middlebrow genre, and although the music becomes a little less pigeon-holed from figure 93, the movement as a whole ends just 16 bars later on a distinctly "easy-listening" added sixth chord on E.

What subject-position does this music project? All of the music for this ballet (which dates from 1928 and was revised by Stravinsky in 1947) plays with more or less highbrow and more or less historically distant styles but does so for the most part with a degree of innovation that keeps the music in a clearly referential but nonetheless "authentic" domain. But this section from the Coda (which is actually not the end of the work—it is followed by a final movement entitled "Apotheosis"), particularly in the context of the more angular music that immediately precedes it, suddenly seems to plunge into parody. As with other examples discussed in this chapter, it is the explicit parading of musical conventions in an untransformed manner, but framed in such a way as to make them the *subject matter* of the musical discourse rather than its *means,* that brings about this sudden change. I find most of the music of the ballet both attractive and rather standoffish in its engagement with "other music"—but at this point in the Coda my own reaction

Example 4.6   Figure 89 to one bar before figure 93 of the Coda
from Stravinsky's ballet *Apollon Musagète*.

is a variety of "you cannot be serious" amusement (that Stravinsky should go this far) mixed with a degree of puzzlement about just what kind of game this is supposed to be. Is it a "commentary"? Or a bit of gratuitous parody? Or a simple indulgence and not a game at all? Or is there some kind of dramatic or narrative motivation for it? Or has Stravinsky simply "lost the plot"?

My final example comes from a Haydn string quartet movement. Haydn's well-known musical jokes are often the result of a deliberate thwarting, or manipulation, of listeners' expectations. At the end of the finale of the quartet in B♭ Major Op. 33 no.2, for example, the rather banal and conventional rondo theme is deconstructed, first by introducing "foreign material" (four inter-jected bars of apparently unrelated *adagio* material); and then by splitting the theme into single phrases separated by bars of silence so that it becomes increasingly difficult to know when the music will stop—or whether it has already. Listening becomes self-con-scious, and one is aware of the manipulative possibilities of musi-cal material. But a more ambiguous example, which has similar-ities with both the Zappa and Stravinsky examples, is the slow movement of the quartet in C Major, Op. 54 no. 2. This short movement (just 35 bars long) is based on an eight-bar chorale-like melody in pure crotchets, which is first presented unadorned, and then with what is effectively a highly embellished *obbligato* part in the first violin. The movement is in C minor (with a short epi-sode in the relative major), and the first violin part makes use of every kind of ornamental effect to squeeze out the pathos in this basically simple material. The ornamentation is in the domain of time as well as pitch, with frequent repetitions of a single pitch (as many as 13 in a row) functioning like an early Baroque *trillo*, written-out accelerandos and juxtapositions of duplets, triplets, and quadruplets combined with liberally applied appoggiaturas, chromatic passing notes and runs, and drawn-out suspensions. As an illustration, example 4.7 shows a short and characteristic pas-sage from the middle of the movement. The result for the move-ment as a whole is a rather extravagant semi-improvised quality,

Example 4.7   Bars 21–24 of the Second Movement of Haydn's String
Quartet in C major, Op. 54 no. 2.

the intensity of which seems odd squeezed into such a short time
frame—particularly as it seems to emerge in an almost unmotivated manner from the very restrained eight-bar opening. As if
to reinforce this incongruous character, the movement ends with
a pause on the dominant, and then moves straight into a rather
plain and muted minuet in C Major (the key of the quartet as a
whole), as if the impassioned slow movement was music that had
wandered in from some other context.

What is the subject-position in this music, and how is it articulated? The material is presented in a manner that hovers between
"heartfelt authenticity" and parody, and—as with Zappa's guitar
solo—this ambivalence seems to come out of a collision between
convention and excess. The simplicity of the opening eight-bar
chorale, with its unbroken crotchet movement, narrow register,
and highly predictable move from tonic to dominant,[8] all specify the conventions of the tonal/metric tradition. This plain and

conventionally organized eight-bar period underlies the rest of the movement, on top of which is superimposed the highly articulated first violin part—and this is where the ambivalence lies. Either this can be heard as genuinely impassioned outpouring—impassioned because it uses all those *Affektenlehre* and *Sturm und Drang* devices that can be found in a more clear-cut context in other works by Haydn and his contemporaries and predecessors; or it is a parody of that same aesthetic, conveyed by the excess of means over ends. The movement seems too insubstantial, the opening eight-bar period too much a caricature of a gloomy chorale, and the extravagant violin part seems to emerge in too unexpected and unmotivated a manner, and to be laid on too thick, to be taken seriously. Suddenly the music seems to be a rather irreverent joke, emphasized by its juxtaposition with the two more worldly major-mode movements that surround it.

The ambiguity of this movement's subject-position as I have argued it here points to two factors that have not been directly addressed so far. The first is the effect that performance can have on subject-position: I can imagine this music being played either in a relatively restrained manner that might minimize the sense of "excess" and ironically emphasize a more passionate and "authentic" subject-position. Equally, a deliberately mannered performance might bring out the potential for this to be heard as parody. In a tradition where the distinction can be drawn between works and performances, this indicates the potential for performers to mediate subject-position. For the Zappa guitar solo, by comparison, the distinction makes little sense—though there is scope for a cover version (for instance by a Zappa tribute band, of which there are quite a few) to adopt a less ironic approach to the material than I have suggested is the case in Zappa's own performance.

The second factor is the reciprocal relationship between the musical material and the (empirical) listener, a consideration that is much more central to the ecological approach. My discussion of the musical examples in this chapter has made no reference to any specific listeners, but it is also apparent that for most music there is more than one way to interpret the subject-position and that the outcome is determined by the listener's specific capacities, concerns, past experience, and so on. In short, the idea that a strict separation can be maintained between subject-position and "empirical subjects" (to refer back to Johnston's distinction at the start of this chapter) is brought into question. The fundamental principle in the ecological approach presented in chapter 1 is that perception is a reciprocal relationship between perceivers and their environments, cospecified by the attributes of both. In the case of the Haydn quartet movement, my hearing of the subject-position in this music as "joking" rather than "serious" is a function of my attention to certain attributes of the music rather than others. It is inevitable that others hear the same sounds in a different way. This observation is nothing new—it is part of the criticism (made by DeNora 2000, among others) that a good deal of musicology discusses musical meaning as if it were a generally shared and self-evident property *of the music*, when in fact it is almost invariably the specific interpretation of one person (the author). DeNora argues that this concealed authoritarianism pays no attention to the musical meanings that arise out of the ways in which people use music in their lives: it is an armchair hermeneutics that ignores unpredictable practical reality.

The problem seems insoluble: at the extremes, one either has to adopt an entirely empirical approach, assessing any and every interpretation against what real listeners hear (and who would those listeners be? how many of them would you ask? what if every one of them heard something different?); or one sticks with what DeNora has depicted as an essentially authoritarian approach in which authors "naturalize" their interpretations by presenting them as self-evident or inherent and erase themselves from the account. There is, however, a middle way between the outright empiricism of an ethnomethodological approach, and the potential authoritarianism of a hermeneutic approach—and that is to combine interpretation with the attempt to ground the analysis in perceptual principles, as I have tried to do here. The aim is not to claim some kind of ultimate perceptual authority for whatever interpretation is proposed, since the perceptual principles seldom, if ever, lead to a single outcome. But consideration of perceptual principles does have the capacity to define an area of *possibilities* within which different empirical individuals may take up their own particular position, and can also help to explain why it is one area of meanings, rather than another, that is specified in a given musical example. The problem is part of the wider debate about music's autonomy: the idea that music is an object, and an object that can be considered in terms of its own inherent principles, independently of the people that engage with it, the history that it shares, or the circumstances in which it is encountered. It is this question, and the perspective on it that an ecological approach can provide, that forms the focus of the next chapter.

Summary

Ecological theory explicitly recognizes the mutualism of perceivers and their environments; one component of that mutualism is the way in which a perceiving subject takes up a stance in relation to the objects of perception. In everyday life, the perception-action cycle is usually so seamless that there may be little need or opportunity for perceivers to become aware of their subject-position in relation to the world. As I look around the keyboard and screen of my computer and move my hands and fingers to type this text, I have only a sense of what I might call my "instrumental" engagement with the immediate environment. The subject-position of everyday life is overwhelmingly one of transparently active engagement. But many aesthetic objects and circumstances change this seamless state of affairs by radically limiting the perceiver's capacity to intervene in, or act upon, the immediate environment in a free-flowing manner. Under these circumstances, perceivers may become much more aware of their *perspective* on the objects of perception.

Part of that perspective is utterly individual—the product of an individual perceiver's skills, needs, preoccupations, and personal history. But an important component is also built into the material properties of the object of perception, and is therefore a shaping force (at least potentially) on *every* perceiver. This is what is captured by the term "subject-position," which, paraphrasing Johnston (1985), can be defined as the way in which music solicits, demands even, a certain closely circumscribed response from the listener by means of its own formal operations. This chapter has argued that there is a way to address the idea of subject-position in both instrumental music and text-based music, and that this focus is a fruitful and productive way both to direct an analysis of musical materials and to enquire about the meanings of those materials. The perceptual framework within which the analysis has been carried out is a way to understand the relationship between musical materials and social meaning—not through the semiotic language of "codification," but through the perceptual principle of "specification." An advantage of this is that the arbitrariness and abstraction of codification is replaced (in ecological theory) by the realism and directness of perception, restoring the connection between aesthetic and practical consciousness.

5 ～

Autonomy/Heteronomy
and Perceptual Style

The last five chapters have discussed how musical meaning can be understood from an ecological perspective and have explored some aspects of subjective experience in listening. The perceptual meaning of sounds, understood as the way in which sounds specify their sources and in so doing afford actions for the perceiver, is the central principle in this approach. Chapter 1 discussed how this requires the concept of "source" to be developed and extended so as to include the culturally specific structural principles and cultural contexts within which music arises, as well as the more obvious sources of place, instrument, physical action, and so on. The virtual sources of sounds have also been discussed in connection with the way in which motion and agency may be specified in sound, and the preceding chapter discussed the idea that musical meaning can encompass both what is specified and the perspective on what is specified (encapsulated within the term subject-position).

The examples that have been used to illustrate these ideas have in many cases either consisted of imagined short sound clips, or have been of a kind where the relationship between sounds and what they specify has clearly led beyond the confines of the music itself—to a world of physical actions and bodily movement, other musical styles, dramatic or narrative context, ideological allegiances, commercial considerations, gender, politics. The passage from the Mozart C major String Quintet (K515) in chapter 3, and the Stravinsky and Haydn examples in the last chapter, have taken the discussion in a more "canonical" direction, but otherwise the discussion of musical meaning has steered clear of the so-called absolute and autonomous music of the Western tradition and the structural listening with which it is associated. Is this because an ecological approach has little to say about this music and the tradition to which it belongs? Does this music really represent a break with, and perhaps a challenge to, the explanatory value of an ecological approach?

Since the idea of music's autonomy has been a central, perhaps *the* central, construct around which the practices and discourse of Western art music have revolved for more than two centuries, it is important to consider what the ecological approach has to say about this tradition and the repertory of music with which it is primarily associated. In this chapter I present two approaches: one considers the way that ecological principles can explain structural listening and the autonomous tradition in their own terms; the other questions the idea of musical autonomy while at the same time recognizing the pervasive influence of this cultural construct, and the listening practices to which it has given rise. Many authors (e.g. Adorno 1976; Subotnik 1988; McClary 1991; Goehr 1992; Kramer 1995; Chua 1999; D. Clarke 2003) have pointed to various different ways in which the ideology of autonomy has been falsely and unsustainably asserted or assumed. If the conclusion drawn from this literature is that musical autonomy is an illusion, that "neither music nor anything else can be other than worldly through and through" (Kramer 1995: 17), then there is simply no issue with which the ecological approach needs to engage. But this is too literal-minded and naïve as a conclusion: however unsustainable it might be in principle, the *idea* of musical autonomy, and of a particular listening attitude in relation to that autonomy, is still a powerful social construct, and one which has important consequences for the ways in which people listen—or perhaps think that they *should* listen—within concert culture.

As already indicated (and see also Bohlmann 1999; Samson 1999; Whittall 1999; and Green 2005), a great deal has already been written about autonomy from the perspectives of musicology and aesthetics; my intention is not to add to that diverse body of writing. The overriding aim of this book is to consider music from a perceptual perspective, and it is within that overall aim that I consider musical autonomy: how ideas about music's autonomy have influenced listening; what kinds of perceptual opportunities and challenges are offered by the music that is most closely associated with the "autonomous tradition"; and how the particular type of subjective experience that is associated with that tradition might be explained within ecological theory. In short, what is it like to listen to music *as if it were autonomous*, and can ecological theory help to explain that experience?

Autonomy, Heteronomy, Absolute Music

The term autonomy, which in a literal sense means self-government or self-determination, as applied to music conveys the idea of a system that operates according to self-sufficient internal principles—a kind of idealized and hermetic formalism. The word can be used both in relation to claims about particular pieces of music, and also as a description of a listening attitude which might be adopted to almost any music. Mozart's string quintet in G Minor K. 516, for example, might be analyzed as an autonomous *work*;[1] or the kind of listening attitude implied by Felix Salzer's analyses of a wide range of classical music (Salzer 1962), or Walter Everett's voice-leading analyses of the Beatles' music (Everett 1999), might be described as autonomous, or structural, *listening.*[2] A radical separation of object from subject is implied by this distinction—as if some music simply *is* autonomous irrespective of the listener's attitude, and that some listening simply *is* autonomous, irrespective of the music. Such a stark distinction is unsustainable, but it helps to identify the close correspondence between the ideas of autonomy and structural listening: autonomous works are those for which the logic of structural integration predominates, and autonomous listening is the kind of listening that follows the structure of an individual work.

This might be regarded as the "positive" definition of autonomy. The self-sufficiency of autonomous systems, however, means that they are isolated, cut off from outside influence or input, blind and deaf to their context and environment, unable to exert any practical influence on the world—and it is this, rather than the idea of self-regulation, that has led to the various critiques of autonomy in more recent musicology. As David Clarke (2003: 159–160) puts it, "The concept of musical autonomy has been having a hard time of it lately," attacked from various directions:

> It is bourgeois and hegemonic: it wants to present its
> socially and historically specific paradigm as universal and
> as the measure against which all other musics are evaluated.
> . . . It is reifying and atrophying: its promotion of music
> as meaningful purely in its own terms, allegedly floating
> free from historical and social contingencies, underwrites
> a canon of putatively timeless masterworks—the fossilized
> museum culture of classical music. It is patriarchal and sex-
> ist: until recently this canon has deflected both feminist
> critique and female participation because, on the one hand,
> its music, putatively formed only out of its own stuff, denies
> the influence of anything so worldly as gender . . . ; while,
> on the other hand, in the record of actual social practice, the
> principal genres of autonomous music—symphony, sonata,
> string quartet—and their associated aesthetic of greatness,
> have been the prerogative of male composers.

Heteronomy is a much less widely used term in discussions of music, though Whittall (1999) is an exception, and the asymmetry is interesting: while it has seemed reasonable to claim, or imagine, the possibility of autonomous works, even if it might prove difficult to produce definitive examples, the opposite extreme (pieces of music which have no definable internal structural relationships and are defined only by context) has seemed harder even to assert, let alone exemplify. In fact, both ends of the spectrum from complete independence to complete dependency are equally unsustainable.

Musical autonomy is powerfully associated with the idea of absolute music for obvious reasons: when music involves words, is integrated with images, dance, drama, or programmatic narratives, it manifestly makes connections with a world outside the work. When music is distanced from those attributes, as in the instrumental concert music of the Western tradition, claims have been made for its absoluteness—a historical change that is closely associated with the development of the concert as an institution.[3] It was in the half-century from 1780 to 1830 that a decisive transformation took place in aesthetic attitude, with the rise of the idea of musical absolutism, as well as the elevated and revered cultural position in which it was placed—though the music to which that attitude applied extended much further back, to Bach and beyond. As an example of the quasi-religious character of musical experience fostered by the aesthetic of absolute and autonomous music, Dahlhaus (1989) quotes from a novella by Wackenroder first published in 1797:

> When Joseph was at a grand concert he seated himself in a
> corner, without so much as glancing at the brilliant assembly
> of listeners, and listened with precisely the same reverence
> as if he were in church—just as still and motionless, his eyes
> cast down to the floor. Not the slightest sound escaped his
> notice, and his keen attention left him in the end quite limp
> and exhausted. (Wackenroder, cited in Dahlhaus 1989: 94)

Cook (1998) and Cook and Dibben (2001) provide examples of paintings from the early nineteenth century in which listeners are depicted with this religious demeanor, often with their eyes closed, in both public and more domestic musical contexts. As Dahlhaus points out, "The 'religion of art' proclaimed by Wackenroder . . . forms one of the historical prerequisites for that intense mode of perception that represents the subjective correlate to absolute instrumental music with its claims to artistic autonomy" (Dahlhaus 1989: 95).

This concern with music as a "special place" to visit, an idealized domain with its own internally coherent principles, is a principal reason why by the mid- to late-nineteenth century it had become the custom to play pieces of music in their entirety, with the movements in the order specified by the composer, and observing repeats. In the late eighteenth and earlier nineteenth centuries it had been common to present music in a much more informal and fragmentary fashion, with individual movements scattered around the concert program. The rise of the "work concept" (Goehr 1992; Dahlhaus 1987), the idea that pieces of music are integrated objects, closely identified with their scores, is as central a feature of this historical development as the invention of the public concert.

Like Dahlhaus, Chua (1999) argues that the idea of absolute music was an invention of the early nineteenth century, and that along with its absoluteness came claims for its ineffability. If absolute music consists of abstract structural units, then it must either have no meaning, or else a meaning that is similarly abstract, absolute, and intangible. And if musical meaning is abstract, absolute, and ineffable then it is only a very short step to claims of universality and mystery, and thus to the quasi-religious character of nineteenth and twentieth century concert listening practices, documented by Johnson (1995) in his history of listening in Paris. Although it would be wrong to attribute such a major cultural shift to the music of a single composer, Beethoven's music seems to have played a particularly important role because of the seriousness with which it was greeted, and the seriousness of intent and structural integration that it was thought to embody. The new attitude, however, was soon applied retrospectively to a great deal of other music, as illustrated by the "re-discovery" and canonization of Bach's music by Mendelssohn and others in the 1830s.

Autonomy and Ecology

By definition, the concepts of ecology and autonomy are fundamentally incompatible. Ecology is the study of *the relationships between* organisms and their environments, and autonomy is the state of independent self-sufficiency—of a system subject only to its own laws or principles. Within the framework of ecology, autonomy is therefore an impossible state: organisms and environments are *always* in a condition of mutual dependence; to isolate either one is to destroy the whole and with it any hope of understanding it *as* a whole.

What is at issue, however, is how ecological theory might help to explain how listeners hear and understand the meaning of music that belongs to a cultural tradition of autonomy; or how ecological theory might help to understand the particular listening attitude that is based on the idea of autonomy. In a paper on the ecological approach to auditory event perception, Gaver (1993a: 1–2) draws a distinction between two ways of listening:

> Imagine that you are walking along a road at night when you hear a sound. On the one hand, you might pay attention to its pitch and loudness and the ways they change with time. You might attend to the sound's timbre, whether it is rough or smooth, bright or dull. You might even notice that it masks other sounds, rendering them inaudible. These are all examples of *musical listening,* in which the perceptual dimensions and attributes of concern have to do with the sound itself . . .

On the other hand, as you stand there in the road, it is likely that you will not listen to the sound itself at all. Instead, you are likely to notice that the sound is made by an automobile with a large and powerful engine. Your attention is likely to be drawn to the fact that it is approaching quickly from behind. And you might even attend to the environment, hearing that the road you are on is actually a narrow alley, with echoing walls on each side.

This is an example of *everyday listening*, the experience of listening to events rather than sounds. (Emphasis in original)

Gaver equates musical listening with an attitude of autonomy—attending to the qualities and properties of sounds in themselves, and their purely sonorous relations with one another. By contrast, everyday listening involves detecting the objects and events in the world that are specified by sounds.

A number of other authors writing from an ecological perspective have taken the same approach, and this constitutes the first way in which ecological theory can be applied to autonomous music and autonomous listening: musical listening is structural listening, and structural listening can be understood as the perception of musical event structures specified by sound. Balzano (1986) for example, in a chapter that explicitly adopts an ecological approach while proclaiming a structuralist orientation in its title ("Music perception as detection of pitch-time constraints"), equates music perception with a thoroughly autonomous perspective. The chapter starts:

The theory and experiments to be presented in this chapter are consequences of a view of music as *constrained pitch-time structures*. Perceiving music is regarded as a process of detecting constraints; more properly, a process of detecting the structures created, or made perceptually available, by the presence of such constraints. (Balzano 1986: 217; emphasis in original)

In a broadly similar fashion, Jones and Hahn (1986) have discussed scale structure from an ecological perspective; Nonken (1999) has analyzed music by New Complexity composers (including works by Dillon, Ferneyhough, and Finnissy) using ecological principles; and, as mentioned in chapter 1, Dowling and Harwood (1986) have used the idea of invariants within an explicitly ecological framework to discuss the ways in which listeners recognize the transformation and return of structures in individual pieces, and within and across repertories. In all these cases, the authors present pieces of music, or sometimes whole repertories or styles, as environments in which sounds specify musical events at a variety of levels of structure— from single pitches, to motifs, themes, scale structures, metrical structures, rhythmic gestures, tonal regions, and much more.

This raises interesting empirical questions about how structures of this kind are specified in sound. What are the invariants that specify a cadence in a particular repertory? Or a key? Or a metrical structure? A great deal of research in music perception has tackled similar questions but, as I have already discussed, predominantly from a perspective that pays very much less attention to invariants in sound (i.e. to the regularities of the sound itself) and much more to the construction of internal representations of one sort or another. Rather than focusing on the inferred presence of internal representations, an ecological approach within the framework of autonomy has the advantage of paying careful attention to the specific attributes of musical sound understood in relation to the capacities of listeners. So although much of the book so far has been concerned with drawing attention to what else *apart* from structure is specified by the sounds of music, it is important to recognize that musical structure *is* something to which listeners can and do pay attention. From an ecological perspective, absolute and autonomous music can be understood as the ways in which musical sounds specify musical structures for listeners.

From a broadly ecological perspective, structural listening is peculiar in encouraging the listener to turn away from the wider environment in searching for meaning. It is therefore worth considering the circumstances that give rise to it. At the risk of creating artificial divisions, I will consider four broad factors that play a part: (i) the listening environment; (ii) the relationship between perception and action; (iii) the compositional characteristics of the music; and (iv) the predispositions or habits of listeners. The first of these, the listening environment, is perhaps the most obvious and crudely determining factor: a traditional aural training or analysis class may specifically *require* students to listen in a structurally focused manner; and, by contrast, in shops, restaurants, clubs, cars, and stations it would be unusual and perhaps difficult and disruptive to pay the kind of focused attention to the sounds themselves that structural listening demands. In part this distinction simply maps onto the continuum between more narrowly (autonomous) and more broadly (heteronomous) focused attention—but that is certainly not the whole story. The kind of listening which takes musical sound as the starting point for a "thought-ful" exploration of any one of a huge potential variety of connected domains (cultural connections, personal memories, other music, unresolved problems, fantasies, inventions . . .) may also be highly integrated and intensely concentrated—but not directed solely at musical structure. To submit to the discipline of the musical structure has become the norm of both musical academia and (in milder form, perhaps) the concert hall—and the result is a style of listening that has technical focus, specificity, and adherence to the particular work as virtues. But it is a considerable leap from recognizing those attributes to claiming that this is the only way really to experience music.

> Submissive listening, which certainly occurs, at least sporadically, at least with certain kinds and examples of music, can be challenged as an instituted norm. Is my not listening that way really a 'deviation'? Am I failing to experience the music when I vary my attention level or simply let it fluctuate, when I interrupt a sound recording to replay a movement or a passage, when I find myself enthralled by a fragment of

a piece that I hear on my car radio without losing concentration on the road, when I intermittently accompany my listening by singing under my breath or silently verbalizing commentary on what I hear, when I perform some part of a piece in my mind's ear, perhaps vocalizing along, and perhaps not? (Kramer 1995: 65)

Just as concentrated listening (or "submissive" listening as Kramer calls it) can be diverted in unexpected directions, so too a listener can be unexpectedly and suddenly drawn *into* some music that until then had been paid more distracted and heteronomous attention—as, for instance, when telephone hold music actually engages your undivided attention rather than being just a sound to fill the waiting. Perhaps the most significant factor in the listening environment, therefore, is the ideological component: the cultural assumption expressed in countless books, magazines, and CD liner notes, radio programs and representations on film and TV, and integrated into formal and informal aspects of music education, that "proper" listening takes a particular form. Stereotyping it, this "particular form" of listening is silent, stationary, uninterrupted, ears glued to the musical structure and eyes closed. It hardly needs pointing out how uncharacteristic this actually is of most people's listening habits.

The second factor in autonomous listening (and one already touched on elsewhere) is the relationship between perception and action. As the ecology of perception emphasizes, perception and action are in reciprocal relationship with one another, such that perception leads to action and action modifies perception. Hearing a sound, I turn my head, or step forward, or cup my hand to my ear: I explore the source of the sound, and in doing so I change the way that I perceive it (it gets louder or softer, clearer or more filtered, I see what is making the sound). But in the circumstances of concert culture, this perception/action cycle is partially disengaged: within tight limits of tolerance, I can turn my head, or crane my neck to try to see who or what is making the sound, or cover my ears. But etiquette prohibits a more thorough and active exploration—however curious I might be about how, or by whom, those sounds have been made, or what dangers or possibilities those sources might afford. Recorded sound makes the disengagement of perception from action both more and less acute: the absence of the *actual* means by which the sounds have originally been made (performers, instruments, spaces) makes it futile to explore the *apparent* sound source: I discover nothing more about the music by peering at my hi-fi, or picking up a loudspeaker, or moving around the room. All of these actions are permitted by the less constrained circumstances of listening at home, but they are ecologically ineffectual. In another way, however, recordings do restore some of the link between perception and action. If a sound on a recording is intriguing, puzzling, or exciting, I can stop the music and play it again, or increase the volume if I feel that I haven't quite caught it, or increase the left channel if that's where it seemed to be, or look at the liner notes in hope of enlightenment. This relationship between perception and action is more remote than when I hear an unexpected sound from somewhere, turn my head towards it, and walk over to investigate; but it is a kind of perception/action cycle nonetheless.

The self-consciousness of human beings means that more than any other living organism they have developed the capacity to move towards "autonomy of consciousness"—the capacity to be (or imagine themselves to be) cut off from the world. Aesthetic objects often disrupt the normal relationship between perception and action, an enforced disengagement that is characteristic of many art forms: paintings may show scenes and objects, but without the third spatial dimension that would afford active exploration; sculptures are made with materials and techniques that invite physical contact, but which you are not allowed to touch; photographs show objects, events, and people into whose timeframe and space you cannot enter; plays and films exclude you from action with which you nevertheless engage at a distance.[4] Everyday, engaged, practical perception is replaced by disengaged, contemplative perception.

Unable to explore and engage with the environment in a literal sense, listeners in conventional concert circumstances may either quickly become bored and alienated or be drawn into a different kind of awareness in which enforced passivity engenders aesthetic contemplation,[5] within which a kind of sublimated and internalized exploration can go on.

One of the consequences of this contemplation is a change of attention from what to do about sounds (or sights) to how they work or are constructed. A picture is both a scene and a surface, and its fascination and particular character lies in that duality. Looking at an engraving by Dürer, for example, I am both aware of the objects and people portrayed (the disconsolate-looking angel in the foreground of his engraving "Melancholia," from 1514, for example), and also the means by which those objects are represented (the way in which the folds and texture of the angel's robe are conveyed simply by black lines on the paper). My attention is drawn to these means because I cannot simply reach out and explore that robe by touching it—because I am obliged to "stop," consider, and contemplate.[6] When I listen to someone in a concert playing a Haydn piano sonata, I am (or can be) aware both of the instrumental and structural events that are taking place (on the one hand the physical piano; and on the other the motifs, sections, rhythmic patterns, harmonic directions, etc.) and the means whereby those events are conveyed (the particular sound of the instrument, the nuances of timing, the detail of articulation and pedaling, and so on). In a similar fashion, when I hear the sound of the preacher's voice in Steve Reich's tape piece *It's gonna rain* (Reich 1965), I first hear someone saying something (I hear words in the English language and their semantic content, as well as the voice in which they are being delivered), but as the tape loop is repeated and layered, my attention gets drawn to the particular character of the sounds themselves—their texture, timbre, rhythm, and pitch. Contemplation leads towards a sense of "things in themselves"— and hence autonomy.

The third factor contributing to a sense of autonomy is the particular character of the musical material. It is a basic principle of the ecological approach that the specific character of perception is codetermined by the capacities and needs of the perceiver, and the opportunities of the environment. Different music, in other words, affords autonomous listening to varying degrees in relation to the perceptual capacities of the listener. The music that affords autonomous listening most obviously is the music of the Western tonal/metric tradition—the music within whose historical development the very idea of autonomy arose.

What characteristics of the musical material afford and elicit this particular kind of auditory engagement? By definition, the music must be unified and structurally integrated, since that is what autonomy ("regulated by its own principles or laws") means—though not every principle of compositional unification or integration will necessarily engage listeners' perceptual capacities. In a paper that discusses compositional systems in the light of general cognitive constraints, Lerdahl (1988) presents one approach to this issue. While his own aim is to argue for the merits of a close fit between what he calls "compositional grammar" (the principles by which composers structure their material) and "listening grammar" (the principles according to which listeners recover underlying structural organization from the musical surface), his discussion can also be understood as an attempt to define the conditions that lead to optimal structural listening of a particular (hierarchical) kind. The basis for this lies in two "aesthetic claims," presented at the end of his chapter: that "The best music utilizes the full potential of our cognitive resources" (Lerdahl 1988: 255) and that "The best music arises from an alliance of a compositional grammar with the listening grammar" (256). The main body of the article consists of a discussion of the cognitive constraints within which musical materials must operate if they are to give rise to structures that are accessible to listeners. These include quite general constraints (e.g. that the musical surface should be capable of being parsed into discrete events, and that these events should be susceptible to hierarchical organization) and more specific constraints relating to particular domains of musical structure (e.g. that pitch space should be organized according to the principle of octave equivalence, and that the octave should be divided into equal parts). Musical structures that adhere to these and the other constraints will be perceptually compelling for listeners, with the result that compositional organization (immanent structure) will be mirrored by the representation in a listener's mind. The consequence is idealized structural listening, and Lerdahl's constraints can be understood as specifying the conditions that must be met if a listener is to recover the structure of the music from its sounding surface. Leaving aside Lerdahl's assertion that the structure perceived by a listener should correspond as closely as possible to the composer's compositional strategy, and allowing therefore for the recovery of structures of which the composer might have been unaware, the rather limited conception of structure adopted by Lerdahl can be criticized (e.g. Boros 1995; Croft 1999; Dibben 1996). Nonetheless, Lerdahl's article, along with the more general tonal theory from which it comes (Lerdahl and Jackendoff 1983; Lerdahl 2001) and the atonal extension to it (Lerdahl 1989), can be seen as provocative attempts to define the material attributes of music that affords structural listening.

The fourth factor is individual predisposition. This is a difficult one about which to make specific and concrete statements, because empirical evidence for people's predispositions as listeners, or what might be called their listening styles, is scant or nonexistent. I will therefore do little more than indicate the involvement of this factor, and briefly discuss two rather different attempts at a typology of listening.

The literature of both fiction and nonfiction provides innumerable personal accounts of people's real or imagined listening styles and constitutes a fascinating window onto the enormous range of listening experiences and listening attitudes. Zbikowski (2002) uses Proust's vivid fictional account of Charles Swann's musical listening from *A la recherche du temps perdu* as the starting point for his discussion of musical understanding and as an illustration of the way that "vague and unformed impressions" (325) develop into active understanding and musical conceptualization. Subotnik, on the other hand, in her critique of structural listening (Subotnik, 1988), claims that the kind of listening which was expected of her, and in which she was trained as a student, left deeply ingrained habits of structural listening—giving the impression that she is as much imprisoned by those habits as enabled by the specific skills that they embody. Brian Eno makes it clear (Eno 1996) that he deliberately cultivates a "distractible" listening attitude, in which he is as happy to be sidetracked by his own thoughts, triggered by the music, as he is to follow the music itself. His own advocacy of Ambient Music in the late 1970s is accompanied by just such a view of listening: "Ambient Music must be able to accommodate many levels of listening attention without enforcing one in particular: it must be as ignorable as it is interesting" (Eno, cited in Toop 1995: 9).

The kinds of account provided by Proust, Subotnik, and Eno make no attempt to be systematic. By contrast, Adorno's (1976) listening typology, though utterly and unapologetically without any empirical foundation, is a striking and iconoclastic attempt to classify different listening attitudes. It is based on the premise that varieties of listening must be understood in relation to the demands of the musical material—and in this sense the whole classification occupies a space that is firmly anchored to the principles of musical autonomy and structural listening. Adorno's types range from the "expert listener," vanishingly rare and nearly always a professional musician, to the "entertainment listener," for whom music is "a comfortable distraction," and who uses music as an emotional trigger and as a kind of sport. "The structure of this sort of listening is like that of smoking," writes Adorno: "We define it more by our displeasure in turning the radio off than by the pleasure we feel, however modestly, while it is playing" (15).

Originally published in 1962, Adorno's typology—which he himself presents as a simplified approximation to a set of "ideal types"—was even then reactionary and anachronistic, out of touch with the changing attitudes to listening that were being driven by developments in electroacoustic, experimental, and pop music. His typology gives the impression that listeners are inflexibly branded according to one of the categories, with no recognition that a person might be an "expert listener" in relation to one kind of music and a "culture consumer" (one of Adorno's types) in relation to another: listeners' predispositions or listening styles are portrayed as if they are independent of the musical material. Though he briefly touches on jazz listeners, Adorno's analysis is premised entirely on the values and practices of the Western art music tradition, infused with a deep pessimism about the totalizing domination of the culture industry and the false-consciousness of its "victims." Nonetheless, it is striking that even with his commitment to understanding the socially sedimented nature of musical materials, he presents listening entirely against the backdrop of assumed autonomy: what defines his "expert" and "good" listeners is their capacity to follow the structural logic of music—with a greater or lesser degree of conscious awareness. An engagement with music's social content and context, with its ideological allegiances, and with the cultural work that it performs, are conspicuously absent from any of the listening categories that he describes.

In complete contrast to Adorno, Benjamin (1970), in his much-cited essay "The Work of Art in the Age of Mechanical Reproduction," argues that so-called distracted attention to art works represents an empowering of perceivers who are otherwise held in thrall by the engulfing quality of the autonomous work and the contemplative attitude that it elicits. Mechanical reproduction, by stripping works of their aura and allowing them to become consumable, disposable, repeatable, and transformable, gives them back to their users and frees those users from "submissive listening": "When the age of mechanical reproduction separated art from its basis in cult, the semblance of its autonomy disappeared forever" (Benjamin 1970: 228).

The age of mechanical reproduction brought with it the technology that enabled the creation of acousmatic music, and the second listening typology considered here is that of the acousmatic composer and theorist Pierre Schaeffer. As discussed by Windsor (2000), Schaeffer distinguishes between four kinds of hearing/listening (écouter, comprendre, ouir, and entendre); although the primary purpose of these four categories is a consideration of acousmatic music, the classification is also relevant to a broader context. For Schaeffer, "écouter" is characterized as an indexical mode of listening concerned with identifying the objects and events that are responsible for the sound—the kind of listening that corresponds most closely to Gaver's "everyday" listening. "Comprendre," on the other hand, is the activity of listening to sounds as signs, in which sounds act as the signifiers for signifieds that lie outside the domain of sound—as when a beeper at a crossing signals that it is safe to cross the road. "Ouir" is defined as simply registering that a sound has taken place, that there has been a sonorous event. And finally "entendre" is the kind of listening that pays attention to the qualities of sounds themselves—their timbre, texture, register, loudness, and so on. This is a very different typology from Adorno's, concerned as it is with modes of hearing/listening that can operate to varying degrees, and at different times and circumstances, in any individual, unlike Adorno's person-based approach. Autonomous listening is associated primarily with "entendre," though the symbolic function encapsulated within Schaeffer's definition of "comprendre" could also play a role if the signification that it embraces were generalized to include sign functions within the medium of the musical material itself, referred to as "intramusical semiosis" by authors such as Agawu (1991). As Dibben (2001) points out, the distinction between autonomy and heteronomy (or reference) does not map neatly onto the distinction between Gaver's musical and everyday listening—nor does it sit easily with Schaeffer's four modes. To listen to music as a self-governing structure is neither "entendre," since this seems to emphasize only its sensory character, nor "comprendre," since as Schaeffer himself presents it, this concerns the capacity of sounds to signify beyond the domain of music itself. Although the modes provide a clear way to identify separate components within listening/hearing, the relative prominence of which may help to define different listening attitudes, Windsor (1995) argues that Schaeffer's primary aim in his own writing is to work towards a *prescriptive* approach to listening that relates to the activities of acousmatic composers—not a *descriptive* account of listening more generally.

Finally, and by contrast with both Adorno's polemical approach and Schaeffer's prescriptive agenda, there are a few empirical studies of listening styles. Kemp (1996) discusses studies by Hargreaves and Coleman (1981), Hedden (1973), and Smith (1987), all of which frame their findings in terms of a continuum between structural or syntactic listening on the one hand, and affective or associative listening on the other. Studies by DeNora (2000) and Sloboda, O'Neill, and Ivaldi (2001) have provided insights into the different ways in which people *use* music in their lives, and thus the styles of listening that they tend to adopt. Neither of these studies is intended as any kind of comprehensive survey (DeNora focused on 52 women in two small towns and two big cities in the U.K. and the U.S.A.; and Sloboda, O'Neill, and Ivaldi studied eight students and staff at a university in the U.K.), but they both reveal the tiny proportion of listening that conforms to the attentive and focused autonomous listening model. Overwhelmingly, people listen to music in a far more pragmatic and "instrumental" manner: as a means to achieving or transforming an emotional state, as the stimulus for exercise, as a social facilitator, or as sound to fill an otherwise awkward silence. Sloboda et al. found that at any randomly sampled moment between 8:00 a.m. and 10:00 p.m. there was roughly a 50 percent likelihood that the participants in their study would have heard music in the preceding two hours, but only a 2 percent likelihood that music was the main focus of their attention. The conditions for autonomous listening seem to be vanishingly rare for these individuals.

In case that seems to be a gloomy conclusion, consider the following vividly imagined scene in which Nicholas Spice suggests the redeeming potential of even the most apparently degraded of musical encounters:

> What countless scenes of love and anger and indifference have been enacted against the background of its [muzak's] blithe fatuities? How many moments of emptiness and despair has it redeemed through incongruity? You are alone on a sales trip to Holland, staying in a hotel in Rotterdam. It is November and you're up at 7 a.m. The breakfast room is in a windowless basement. Outside, fog hugs the cobblestones and Dutchmen cycle to work. You sit down at a table covered with a carpet. A young waiter just out of catering school brings you a module of Dutch breakfast: two pieces of currant bread, a jug of hot water already too cold to revive the Lipton's tea-bag in the accompanying cup, a boiled egg—white, tepid and undercooked. No one speaks. The waiter moves about discreetly behind the breakfast hatch clinking tea-cups. Only the occasional pop of vacuum seals on miniature jam pots breaks the silence. You take a bite out of the currant bread which is sweet and unappetising, crack the egg and attempt to spoon the slobbery transparent egg white into your mouth . . . At this point you feel so sad that you do not know where to put yourself. And then you notice the muzak—'songs of time-travel into amniotic bliss', perhaps—and the incongruity of it all tips this moment, which, experienced in complete silence, would be unbearable, into absurdity. A gap opens between you and the music, and into that gap you escape. (Spice 1995: 6)

A number of aspects of this account are striking: its strongly auditory character; the complex and differentiated auditory environment that it conveys; the roving, scanning, and sampling quality of the listening; and the sudden awareness of the muzak with which the extract finishes. The revelatory potential of music is usually associated with attentive structural listening, and with "musical masterpieces": but here it is presented in the context of "distracted" listening to the most utilitarian and commercially compromised of musical materials. The conjunction of context, material, and listening style which opens up Spice's "gap" can take a complementary but no less striking form when "autonomous" listening becomes "distracted": in the middle of a performance (imagine a Haydn piano sonata played in Leeds Town Hall) you suddenly notice how extraordinary and bizarre it is to be sitting with 500 other people in a Victorian building, thirty years after human beings set foot on the moon, paying rapt attention to music written two hundred years ago and played by a man from Manchester wearing nineteenth-century formal clothes.

Music and Transformation: Autonomy Strikes Back

As explored in chapters 3 and 4, the close connection between music and subjectivity is a central component of musical meaning, and one of the particular characteristics of musical autonomy is the specific sense of self that this kind of focused engagement with musical material can elicit. If heteronomous listening has revelatory potential by virtue of the worlds that it brings together, there are others who have argued that it is the capacity of music—listened to autonomously—to set itself *against* the world that endows it with a transforming power. Whittall (1999), for example, in an analysis of a solo flute piece by Elliott Carter, seeks to balance the claims and characteristics of immanent structure with the diversity and complexity of the work's context, references, and influences. But he also asserts that in "linking work to world, it is still the work that dominates, because it represents a triumph over the world: it is a product of the world that transcends its context" (98). It is not surprising, perhaps, that he should give primacy to the work—since this is the writing of a musicologist, not a social historian or cultural theorist. But notice that Whittall argues for the domination of the work not on the grounds of his own particular perspective, but on the more absolute grounds that the work is a "triumph over the world," that it "transcends its context." In one way or another, this is the view of those (perhaps most obviously Adorno) who argue for the critical power of music, for "the possibility that works of art may be defences against the world as much as products of the world" (Whittall 1999: 100).

In a sustained defense of the value of classical music, Julian Johnson (2002) argues for the transforming potential of "music-as-art," as he calls it. While Johnson recognizes that music fulfils a range of functions (as entertainment, as propaganda, as therapy, as a means for coordinated action), music-as-art is distinguished by virtue of its emphasis on formal organization. While sound is common to all these functions, Johnson argues that music-as-art is characterized by the way that, without denying the sensuous qualities of sounds, it uses the structure of sounds as "a vehicle for musical thought"(Johnson 2002: 48). The formal elaboration of sound has the consequence that music-as-art develops its own structural principles, based on their own internal logic and generating and obeying their own historical development—in other words, autonomy. Autonomy provides music-as-art with its distance from the everyday, its ability to transform the everyday and "offer back a refracted version." There, in "the distance between the real everyday and its aesthetic reworking lies art's capacity for critique and utopian suggestion" (49). The dilemma for music-as-art is that the critical opportunity afforded by its removal from the everyday also risks rendering it ineffectual and escapist.

Autonomy is historically linked with absoluteness, and together these project an image of music-as-art that inclines strongly towards abstraction. Johnson argues that absolute music, free of the representational constraints of drama, texts, and images takes on a cognitive, cerebral character. It presents itself "as a special kind of object that, through its internal organization, transcends its thinglike quality by being taken up as thought, as an intellectual or spiritual activity rather than merely a physical, *perceptual,* or sensuous one" (Johnson 2002: 86; emphasis added). But this apparent endorsement of music's abstraction, and the claim for its cognitive character, seems to involve the unwarranted assumption that perception is somehow too mundane, too concerned with pragmatic considerations, to be reconciled with the transcendent character of music-as-art. Johnson's case for the special attributes of music-as-art starts with the statement:

> To talk of art implies the priority of an object over our perception. How people habitually perceive and interpret things is an important question, but it is not ultimately related to the question of art's *potential.* If perception is not shaped by the object, then one is no longer talking about art at all. (51; emphasis in original)

This presents a peculiar view of perception, suggesting that in certain circumstances (and by implication these are "everyday" circumstances) perception might operate in a manner that was independent of its objects. From almost any point of view, but certainly from an ecological perspective, this is untenable: perception always involves the reciprocal relationship between the opportunities of the environment and the capacities of the perceiver. In art as in all other aspects of reality, perception is codetermined by both the organism and its objects, but not necessarily in equal measure. When the "balance" between subject and object emphasizes the familiarity of the object in relation to the perceiver it has an affirmative character; and when it emphasizes the strangeness of the object in relation to the perceiver it has transforming potential, a dynamic that Piaget (e.g. Piaget 1977) encapsulated in the relationship between assimilation and accommodation.

A significant component of music's capacity to engage and transform the listener lies in its power to temporally structure the sense of self. By virtue of its highly organized temporal but non-spatial structure, music provides a virtual environment in which to explore, and experiment with, a sense of identity. Cross (2003) has suggested that music's adaptive significance in human evolution is that it provides a risk-free context in which to experiment with social interactions, and a safe domain within which to learn tolerance of multiple and ambiguous meanings. This suggests that a crucial attribute in being able to experience music-as-art is the capacity to de-center—to take the part of another, to feel what it might be like to take on the "style of subjectivity" (or subjectivities) of, for example, the first movement of the A minor string quartet, Op. 132, by Beethoven. DeNora (2000), in a chapter entitled "Music as a Technology of Self," provides numerous examples of the ways in which listeners report that they use music to enable, stabilize, or explore different aspects of their sense of self. It is clear from these accounts that this is a complex mixture of discovery (as if that subjective attribute was already there in the music, waiting to be "taken on") and projection—the music acting as a pliable substrate able to shape itself to the listener's subjective will, but reflecting back a transformed sense of him- or herself.

If this seems fanciful, consider the more tangible and visible example of human movement in relation to music. The unchoreographed[7] dancing that goes on at clubs, discos, and parties is both an expression of the dancer's sense of self projected *onto* the music, and an exploration of what is *in* the music by means of the self. A dancer's movements are both expressive of what a person thinks the music is "about" (through variations in the size, speed, fluency, diversity, precision, etc. of the movements) and also driven by the material characteristics of the music itself (including its tempo, texture, tonality, rhythmic patterns, and density). In similar fashion, so-called "air guitar" can be understood as performing the same split role: it both expresses the "air" player's subjectivity by means of the music and projects his subjectivity onto the music, enabling the player to achieve a closer and more intense identification with the music through embodied action. Smith (1995), describing a favorite track of his by the English band The Faces, vividly suggests the engagement and identity that this kind of projection or mimicry can afford, and the centrifugal and centripetal power of pop on the psyche:

> When it was loud enough and the bedroom door was shut, I could run with it, over to the mirror, hands shaped around an imaginary guitar, thumb and forefinger of my right hand pressed together and twitching against my thigh while I mouthed lyrics at my reflection.
>
> There is nothing like pop music for getting you out of yourself; but the opposite and equal truth is, there is nothing like pop for centring you *in* yourself. Here's pop, this monumentally outgoing, life-affirming force, proof of the raging heart and the racing pulse. Odd, then, the solipsistic nature of so many of the pleasures you took in it: the bedroom hours . . ., the solo dancing, the mirror miming, the listening through headphones, which is even now my favourite way to hear things, to sink into them, sealed off, so that there's no distraction. At which point, pop was not the soundtrack to your life, it *was* your life. (Smith 1995: 39–40)

Listening while Performing: Perception and Action, Autonomy and Heteronomy

The intense identification with music that Smith describes, the blurring of subject and object, remains tilted towards the object in the circumstances that he describes simply because the object (the recording) is a fixed entity over which the subject (listener) has little or no control. The listening that a *performer* does, however, has the potential to dissolve that subject/object distinction even more radically. In *playing* music, the object really is within the control of the subject, because perception and action—held apart for listeners in concert culture—are in dynamic relation with one another. Different performing contexts give different perspectives on this subject/object dissolution, but Kramer (1995) argues that the solo amateur keyboard player, playing for no-one but him- or herself, represents a special kind of listening and doing—and one which presents a contradictory relationship with autonomy. From one perspective, the solo keyboard player embodies the autonomous ideal, the self-sufficient individual by whose own actions the work is made. "At the keyboard I forget, I am licensed to forget, everything but the music itself" (Kramer 1995: 232). Indeed, perhaps not just licensed to forget but even obliged to forget: playing the keyboard is a demanding skill, and as research on the psychology of attention has shown (e.g. Kahneman 1973), demanding tasks require highly selective focal attention. Kramer may be aware only of "the music itself," in a state of identification with its autonomy, because in a culture that emphasizes fidelity to the work, that kind of highly focused attention is what playing such music requires. Here autonomy links up with subjectivity and consciousness: at those times when a performer's own consciousness/subjectivity seems to be absorbed into the virtual consciousness/subjectivity of "the music," the sense of musical autonomy is strongest.

But as Kramer points out, the hands on the keyboard are also a reminder of music's heteronomy—of its far-from-idealized physicality, as the fingers search for the right notes, trip over themselves to maintain the tempo, or (as Kramer describes himself playing Bach) struggle with awkward trills. These difficulties and resistances are reminders of the physicality and worldliness of making music, and of just how far from an idealized, transcendent "substance" music really is. While historically autonomy may be most powerfully associated with the "great masterpieces" of Viennese Classicism—Beethoven's quartets and piano sonatas, for example—it is these same pieces that confront players with both physical and conceptual resistances to the forgetful state of autonomy that Kramer describes. Unself-conscious, forgetful, and present-centered consciousness, which Csikszentmihalyi has called flow

(Csikszentmihalyi 1990), may be associated not with the uniquely integrated structures that Beethoven's music has come to stand for, but with the more predictable conventions of less remarkable Classical music—where the demands of the material and the skills of the player are more closely matched.

The intimate relationship between perception and action in the ways that players listen takes many forms, depending—among other factors—on the playing circumstances and the specific instruments. To take just two examples, the solitary intensity of keyboard performance that Kramer describes is characterized both by the particular circumstance of an individual playing complete multipart music on his own, and the specific physical characteristics of the instrument in relation to the human body (its separation from the body, the way in which the keyboard mechanism "distances" the hand from the direct means of sound production[8]). In string quartet playing, on the other hand, not only are perceiving and acting distributed around four individuals, but each of those players has a physical relationship with the means of sound production that is very different from the circumstances of keyboard playing. There is a palpable directness in the body's relationship with the means of sound production (fingers on strings, hand on bow), particularly in the production of pitch and tone quality. The way in which the left hand will only move reliably to a place on the string that the ear can hear "in advance"[9] is a compelling illustration of the interdependence of perception and action.

Finally, improvisation involves a kind of listening-while-performing that highlights the relationship between perception and action, and autonomous and heteronomous perspectives, in a particularly acute amnner (see Sudnow 2001). One of the informants in Paul Berliner's seminal research on jazz talks about the physical character of the way he hears and maintains different timing relationships with the beat (before, on top of, and after the beat). As Berliner points out, these distinctions—often imperceptible to a nonspecialist—take on "such tangible qualities that the beat seems a physical object, a palpable force. 'There's an edge I feel when I'm playing walking bass lines on top of the beat. It's like if you're walking into the wind,' Rufus Reid observes poetically, 'you feel a certain resistance when your body is straight, but you feel a greater resistance if you lean into the wind'" (Berliner 1997: 13–14). In the context of group improvisation, the players must all somehow combine that intense physical involvement with their own material while simultaneously remaining open to, and aware of, everything that is going on around them. These competing autonomous/heteronomous demands, and the distributed quality of the resulting listening and playing, are vividly captured in the following passage:

> Although hearing everything over a musical journey represents the ideal, listening is typically a dynamic activity and performers continually adopt different perspectives on the musical patterns that surround them. Their constantly fluctuating powers of concentration, the extraordinary volume of detail requiring them to absorb material selectively, and developments in their own parts that periodically demand full attention, together create a kaleidophonic essence of each artist's perception of the collective performance. Moreover, as suggested above, improvisers sometimes deliberately shift focus within the music's dazzling texture to derive stimulation from different players. Walter Bishop, Jr. can 'zero in on the bass player or the drummer, either one by himself or both together. Or, if the band's a quartet, I can listen in quadruplicate.'
>
> Amid the rigorous operations of listening and responding, the overlapping perceptions of all the players can potentially compensate for any individual's difficulties or divergent viewpoints and bring cohesion to the larger performance. The piano player might hear something in what the soloist is playing that the drummer does not hear at the time, but if the drummer hears the pianist's response to the soloist and he complements the pianist's idea, then what the

drummer plays will also complement 'the whole musical thought of the soloist' (Leroy Williams). (Berliner 1997: 25)

Summary

The ecological approach to perception emphasizes the perceiving organism's adaptation to its environment, and the manner in which perceptual information specifies events in the world. By contrast, the idea of musical autonomy suggests that musical structures are self-sufficient, subject only to their own immanent principles. These two perspectives seem incompatible: does an ecological approach, therefore, have anything to say about this musical tradition, which has occupied such a culturally privileged position? This chapter has addressed the question from two standpoints. First, accepting the idea of autonomy on its own terms, music can be understood as constituting a "virtual world" into which a listener is drawn. An ecological approach can then help to understand the ways in which the events of this virtual world (tonal events, metrical events, textural events, motivic events) are specified in sound. Second, ecological principles can contribute to the critique of autonomy while recognizing the pervasive influence of this cultural construct, and the listening practices with which it is associated. Musical autonomy may be an illusion, but it has given rise to a kind of listening that has particular characteristics and preoccupations. This style of listening arises from the interaction of a number of factors: listening circumstances, the relationship between perception and action, the organization of musical material, and listeners' predispositions. An outline of how some of these factors might operate has been presented, and the relationship between the critical and ideological character of autonomy has been discussed. Finally, the chapter has discussed the particular kind of subjectivity that an autonomous engagement with music—however illusory—can elicit, and the competing demands on a performer's consciousness that listening-while-playing makes.

The next chapter presents a perceptually motivated analysis of a piece of music from the autonomous tradition—the first movement of the A minor string quartet by Beethoven (Op. 132)—to demonstrate the ways in which an ecological approach might cast light on the subjective experience of a style of music that has been regarded by many as decidedly "unworldly."

6 〜

The First Movement of Beethoven's String Quartet in A Minor, Op. 132

What is it like to listen to the first movement of Beethoven's String Quartet in A minor, Op. 132? "What is it like to be a bat?" asks Thomas Nagel in the title of an essay (Nagel 1981) on the impossibility of ever knowing what the subjective experience of another organism might be like. Nagel argues that in trying to imagine what it is like to be a bat, we try to imagine ourselves as small and furry, equipped with wings and echolocation—and end up with a human in bat's clothing, as it were, rather than a bat's mind in a bat's body. In the same way, any attempt on my part to give an account of what it is like to hear this Beethoven quartet movement, and to try to understand *why* it sounds like it does will fall foul of the same problem. The impossibility of adopting a properly bat-like perspective is, of course, of a different order from that of generalizing from my own experience to that of a wider human listenership: nonetheless, the ecological approach presents perception as a mutual relationship between organism and environment, so that every description of perception is therefore specific to an individual's capacities and perspective—even if based in common ecological principles. My approach will be to outline and describe some of the perceptual opportunities that exist in the piece based on my own experience of the music and the writings of others, without prescribing which (if any) of these an individual listener might be aware of—but showing how they can all be understood within the approach developed in this book. My motivation, therefore, is primarily theory-oriented rather than piece-oriented: the music is used to assess the value of an ecological approach for understanding the perception of this kind of music, and the question that runs as a thread through this chapter is "What is there to hear in this movement?"

My approach has quite a lot in common with Hatten's (1994) extensive discussion of Beethoven's music from a semiotic perspective. Hatten combines a discussion of structural and expressive motivations in the semiotics of Beethoven's music in a way that aims at a synthesis of the two and tries to avoid the false dichotomy of "intramusical" and "extramusical."

> I offer a theory that claims to be both structuralist and
> hermeneutic, but that expands the range of these comple-
> mentary approaches. The theory is structuralist in its further
> pursuit of the structure of expression, and hermeneutic in
> its further pursuit of the expressiveness of formal structures.
> (Hatten 1994: 279)

But in two important respects the approach that I present here is significantly different from Hatten's. First, I am principally concerned with contemporary—twenty-first century—listening, while Hatten's aim is explicitly a "historical reconstruction of an interpretive competency adequate to the understanding of Beethoven's works in his lifetime" (Hatten 1994: 3). Not only is the historical perspective significantly different, but so too is Hatten's rather more inclusive term "interpretive competency" by comparison with my own focus specifically on listening. Second, Hatten (following Eco 1977) relies primarily on the principle of correlation between musical materials and "cultural units" (expressive content)—established by conventions of use. The term "correlation" is chosen deliberately to avoid any sense of causality: musical materials have no capacity to determine specific cultural units, they simply float in the same cultural space and can enter into associations that are more or less motivated by a variety of factors. Hatten refers to Gibson's concept of affordance, and indeed distinguishes between a psychological realm in which musical materials have a "pre-stylistic" relationship of affordance with their expressive consequences, and a cognitive realm in which materials are in a stylistically mediated correlation with their expressive counterparts. The approach that I have argued for in this book resists the nature/culture opposition, and the distinction between innate and learned with which this is closely connected, in favor of a unified theory of the environment in relation to perceivers. Lastly, rather than relying on the causally neutral concept of correlation, I argue for the stronger explanatory value of specification and affordance. In short, Hatten's approach to Beethoven's music is historically reconstructive and semiotic, while the discussion presented here is contemporary and ecological.

Beethoven's late quartets, along with the last three piano sonatas, occupy an elevated position within Western art music, and as Chua (1999) has argued, Beethoven's music in general occupies a special place in the development of the idea of absolute music. Certainly this music has been widely discussed as a radical confrontation with its own principles (sonata form, thematicism, the sense of its own musical history) by means of those principles themselves, and in that sense is emblematic of the principle of autonomy. In what follows I will draw on the semiotic analysis of this movement presented by Agawu (1991) but will reinterpret it within a perceptual framework and supplement it with other perspectives. My approach will be to consider the movement from a number of different angles, which, though presented separately, are understood to coexist and to interact in the experience of a listener. No hierarchy of perspectives is implied here, since the sounds of this music (as with any sounds) specify a whole variety of objects or events simultaneously: a sound can be simultaneously the sound of a cello, of Western art chamber music, of a G# rising to an A, of the opening of the first movement of Beethoven's Op. 132 string quartet . . . Every individual listener is more or less attuned to these different opportunities, some of which may be more widespread as learned sensitivities in the general population (most people are probably more likely to hear "cello" than "Beethoven Op. 132"), but this is a matter of differentiated perceptual learning rather than of musical or psychological significance.

Topic Theory

Agawu's 1991 book on the semiotics of Classical music presents the meaning of this repertory as arising out of the relationship between two components of the music: its tonal structure, understood as the elaboration of an essentially beginning–middle–end plan; and the use of a repertoire of musical "topics." The theory of musical topics, developed by Ratner (1980) and used by Agawu, proposes that musical meaning is communicated by means of conventional musical signs, whose signification arises out of their association with particular musical and nonmusical functions: horn calls for hunting, a whole variety of dance rhythms, self-consciously deliberate contrapuntal procedures to convey a "learned style," rapid figuration for "virtuosity" or "brilliance," and so on.

Agawu writes of the first movement of Mozart's String Quintet in C major:

> As a work that embodies a specific historical moment, the first movement of Mozart's C Major Quintet is best understood as partaking of a universe of stylistic signs current in the eighteenth century—signs that formed the listening environment of its composers and listeners, and were used consistently in work after work by Mozart and his contemporaries. This exercise has unearthed a number of references to various dances such as gavotte and bourée, to styles such

as musette and the pastoral, to historical styles such as sensibility and Sturm und Drang, to gestures such as fanfare, and to procedures such as the learned style. By their mere presence, these topical signs embody that historical reality. (Agawu 1991: 98)

Agawu's comment that the work partakes of a universe of stylistic signs that form "the listening environment" of contemporary composers and listeners demonstrates one way in which topic theory can be understood within an ecological approach. Topics, conceived as more or less stable entities in the cultural environment of late eighteenth century and early nineteenth century Europe, are specified by particular invariants (dronelike static harmonic events for the musette; the characteristic rhythmic signature for a gavotte; imitative or species counterpoint for learned style); and the analysis presented here attempts to identify those invariants in the Beethoven movement.

In common with other topic theorists (e.g. Ratner 1980; Monelle 2000), Agawu aims to describe and understand musical meaning in terms of the experiences of listeners contemporaneous with the works analyzed: this is the kind of listening envisaged in his analysis. In order to support that aim, he provides a certain amount of evidence (Monelle considerably more so in his discussion) from documents of the time: a letter from Mozart to his father, for instance, discussing the use of Turkish music and the effect that this will have on the audience. But there is also a subtle shift in both Agawu's and Monelle's accounts from an assumed late eighteenth/early nineteenth century listening competence to the competence and circumstances of present-day listeners. Agawu writes:

The perspective of sonata form is best conceived as the composer's working mechanism and, by transfer, as a comparable background working mechanism for the listener. *We do not listen for sonata form; we simply hear it.* (Agawu 1991: 99; emphasis added)

Although he is writing here of listening competence in regard to tonal structure and large-scale form, rather than sensitivity to topics, the point is the same: the distinction between a reconstructed (and perhaps idealized) eighteenth century listener and the late twentieth century author (and readers) of Agawu's book is blurred. Similarly, Allanbrook (1983), in defining topic in music, makes an alarming assumption for late twentieth century listeners if taken at face value: "In music the term [*topos*] has been borrowed to designate 'commonplace' musical styles or figures whose expressive connotations, derived from the circumstances in which they are habitually employed, *are familiar to all*" (329 n. 4; emphasis added). This is an unrealistic assessment of the listening competence of anything but a very small and specialized subset of late twentieth century listeners, and Allanbrook's subsequent case for the empirical currency of her topics is hardly convincing. Claiming that topical associations are "both natural and historical," she nonetheless argues that "Because of their connections with certain universal habits of human behavior, these *topoi* are also largely in the possession of the opera-going audience today, although modern listeners may not be aware of the source of their particular perceptions" (Allanbrook 1983: 2–3).

Whenever writing about music refers explicitly or implicitly to "what people hear"—in other words whenever it steps outside narrow formalism—it invokes some kind of implied or idealized listener. Sometimes this is explicit, as in Cumming's (2000) recognition of the inevitable subjectivity of writing about music, or Lerdahl and Jackendoff's (1983) statement that their theory is a "formal description of the musical intuitions of a listener who is experienced in a musical idiom" (Lerdahl and Jackendoff 1983: 1). But more often, as discussed by DeNora (2000) and others, it is a hidden assumption that may be used to impose on listeners/readers a hearing which they may regard as anything from revelatory to incomprehensible. Cook (1990) has argued that analytical or critical statements about music can be understood as ways in which the music *might be* heard rather than as descriptions of how music *is* heard, so that Agawu's, Allanbrook's and Monelle's descriptions of the topical meanings of the music they discuss can be understood as recommendations for a way of listening to this repertoire that draws on the musical and, more broadly, cultural context within which this music was created. Such recommendations are benign, but they leave untouched the question of whether this is anything that people actually hear in the music.

An alternative is to approach the matter in a more explicitly empirical manner, as Tagg and Clarida (2003) have done for a selection of film and TV title tunes, or as Krumhansl (1998) has done in relation to the specific music analysed by Agawu. Carried out with a restricted repertory and no more than a sample of listeners, this is a tractable proposition, but any degree of generality makes this an impossible task: the number of more or less distinct repertories, and more or less specialized listener populations, is limitless and overwhelming. Furthermore, any empirical approach is limited to the here and now, and part of the point of Agawu's and Monelle's approaches is to explore what the experience of eighteenth and nineteenth century listeners might have been like. The problem seems particularly acute when music's topical organization is considered, because of the speed with which topical specification can change, and dramatic individual differences in sensitivity and attunement to topics—partly as the result of the huge variety of musical cultures and subcultures to which contemporary listeners belong or are exposed.[1]

By considering what they regard as a more fundamental aspect of musical organization (tonal and rhythmic structures), Lerdahl and Jackendoff tackle the problem of subjective variability in a different way: "Rarely do two people hear a given piece in precisely the same way or with the same degree of richness," they recognize. "Nonetheless, there is normally considerable agreement on what are the most natural ways to hear a piece" (Lerdahl and Jackendoff 1983: 3). Here, perhaps, is one place where psychological and musicological perspectives part company: cognitive psychology has regarded general principles of perception and cognition, which apply with considerable cross-cultural stability to a broad spectrum of humanity, as its primary focus. Consistent with this, Lerdahl and Jackendoff regard the time-span, prolongational, grouping and metric structure of the tonal/metric repertory to be of sufficient generality and cross-cultural stability to apply with some uniformity to most "experienced" listeners. In much the same way, auditory psychologists such as Bregman (1990) and Handel (1989) make this assumption about the perception of "everyday" sounds and speech sounds across an even wider mass of listeners. Musicology, by contrast, takes the cultural specificity of its material (and hence of its interpretations) as a premise—even if that premise is sometimes unacknowledged.

The approach that I adopt in this chapter, therefore, is a compromise. On the one hand it seems perverse to dismiss the relevance of the kinds of topics that Agawu and others identify simply because there may be very few listeners who are sensitive to them: the analyses provided by those authors are themselves testimony to the perceptibility of those features, whether that perceptibility is the *result* of score-based analytical work or the original *motivation* for it. On the other hand, the great majority of twenty-first century listeners are probably not at all attuned to those characteristics of the music, but are attuned to others—by virtue of the significant changes in musical culture and sensibility that have taken place in the two intervening centuries. To confine my account only to the kinds of topics that Agawu and others discuss ignores those other perceptible attributes. Since my principal aim in this chapter is to discuss "what there is to be heard" in this movement, and to explain how it is that those things can be heard, anything that people can and do hear is grist to my mill: analysts, commentators, and most obviously myself. There is no attempt to be "comprehensive" in what follows: my aim is to pick out some of the attributes that I and other people have heard, and to explain what it is about the musical material that makes those things audible.

Topics in Op. 132/I

Topical organization is clearly a striking feature of the Beethoven quartet movement, with contrasting types of material being abruptly juxtaposed in many places. In his own analysis, Agawu identifies nine topics that play a role in the movement, from the "provisional universe of topics" that he assembles to discuss the three chamber works by Haydn, Mozart, and Beethoven that form the core material for his book (see Agawu 1991: 30). These nine topics are: Learned Style, Alla Breve, Fantasy, Cadenza, March, Sensibility, Gavotte, Aria, and Brilliant Style. An example of the learned style is the opening eight bars of the movement and later variants of that material; of cadenza, the rapid figuration in the first violin at bars 9–10; and of aria, the rather stable "theme and accompaniment" that is heard from bar 48 (see example 6.1). The topics that Agawu identifies are derived from late eighteenth and early nineteenth century conventions historically grounded in actual social practices (dancing, hunting, worship, musical institutions—e.g. opera) as well as more abstracted social representations. For the members of a nineteenth century audience, some of the practices which these topics represent were already somewhat historically remote, and for many individuals these topics must have specified experiences which were in a literal sense unfamiliar: there must have been plenty of listeners at the first performance of Op. 132 in 1825 who had never danced a gavotte or composed music in the "learned style," but who were capable of recognizing these for what they are—just as there were plenty of listeners in 1969 who were perfectly able to recognize the "psychedelic" topic in The Beatles's "Lucy in the Sky with Diamonds" without ever having had any experience of LSD themselves.[2] Conventions of use ensure that a certain rhythmic device will specify the gavotte as a "cultural unit" (Eco 1977), or that a particular swirly filtering effect will specify "psychedelia," to suitably attuned listeners. It is plausible that at least some of the listeners at the first performance of Op. 132 in 1825 would have had the specific sensitivity required to identify some or all of Agawu's topics (and possibly others too), and that an important component of their experience of the movement would therefore have been an appreciation of the presentation and interplay of these topics.

To make this a little more concrete, consider the specific appearance of just three of the topics: the learned style of bars 1–8; the gavotte of bars 40–43; and the aria of bars 48–60 (see example 6.1). The semiotic framework within which Agawu works means that he understands and presents topics as signs. But it is equally possible to understand them from a perceptual point of view—and in fact Agawu himself comes very close to this (and in rather ecological language) when he writes that each topic "is a member of a larger topical class that is defined by certain invariant characteristics whose presence alone guarantees the topic's identity. That is, a given topic may assume a variety of forms, depending on the context of its exposition, without losing its identity" (Agawu 1991: 35). The question can therefore be expressed as, "what are the invariants that perceptually specify learned style, gavotte, or aria?" The learned style is specified at the opening of the movement by a number of clear perceptual attributes: the slow and regular note-against-note counterpoint; the complete absence of embellishment or decoration; the measured entries of the four instruments of the quartet; the motivic imitations and re-ordering of elements; and the harmonic pattern of rather conventional small-scale closures— half-bar alternations of a preparatory (tense) chord followed by a resolution, all within a very narrow harmonic region.

The invariants that specify the second topic—the gavotte at bar 40—are straightforwardly rhythmic. In the eighteenth century a gavotte was a dance rhythm in duple meter at a moderate tempo characterized primarily by a pair of upbeats leading to the principal downbeat (Allanbrook 1983: 49–52)—and at the second half of bar 40 into bar 41 this is exactly what is heard, initially in the first violin, and then in the cello and second violin. As with the learned style, the head motif of this topic is presented in a distinct and clearly articulated form, set against the preceding context by

Example 6.1   Bars 1–62 of the First Movement of Beethoven's
String Quartet in A minor, Op. 132.

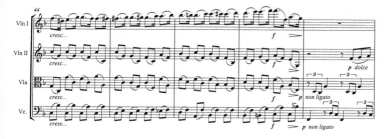

Example 6.1 (*Continued*)

a sudden change in dynamic and texture. As Agawu points out, the pattern of imitations across instruments also gives this passage a quality of learned style, and after just three and a half bars, the topic disappears—abruptly displaced by new material.

My third example from Agawu's analysis is the aria that follows just four bars after the disappearance of the gavotte, at bar 48. This is perhaps the clearest of all the topics presented in this movement, an almost self-consciously stylized "theme and accompaniment" texture in F major, with the viola and cello accompaniment in triplets clearly differentiated from the two statements of the theme (in duplets) in the violins. The properties that define the topic are therefore the differentiation of theme and accompaniment (rhythm and register); the easy vocal quality of the conjunct linear melody which moves primarily in crotchets and quavers; the broken figuration and undifferentiated rhythm of the accompaniment; the conventional harmonic basis; and the regular binary phrase structure. The topic appears just three times in the movement, each time with more or less all of these features intact.

Not all the topics in the movement are as clear as these three. Indeed, the most prevalent topic, the march, is in many ways the least well, and the most variably, specified. Like the gavotte, this topic is primarily specified by rhythmic features: duple meter, no upbeats, and a tendency for undivided main beats and dotted rhythms on the weak beats (cf. Allanbrook 1983: 45–48). The first example of this, at bar 11, specifies the march poorly for a number of reasons: the first main beat is missing (and remains so through much of the movement); the dynamic is quiet and undermines the conventionally more assertive character of the march; and the minor key and conjunct melodic profile are uncharacteristic,[3] as is the thin texture (a high cello line against a single sustained violin note). Although the characteristic alternation of an undivided main beat with a dotted rhythm on the weak beats appears somewhere in the texture for the next six bars, its identity is eroded in bars 18 and 19 as the four instruments converge onto a uniform dotted rhythm on every beat (see example 6.1). The process starts again at bar 23, with the same dissolution into rhythmic uniformity—a pattern that is repeated innumerable times, and in somewhat different ways, throughout the movement. Indeed the march is never properly established in the movement, and many listeners who hear the aria, for instance, as a well-defined element, might remain only dimly aware of the march despite its almost constant, though subliminal, presence throughout the movement.

This, then, provides a brief account of a subset of the topics in the movement, both in terms of their conventional meaning (that is, what they are perceived to *be*) and in terms of some of the perceptual characteristics that may be responsible for their invariant identity. But as already noted, this is an account largely predicated on the kind of listening sensitivity and competence that an experienced listener of about 1825 might have had. What kinds of topics—if any—might a modern-day listener be aware of? As already discussed, this can be regarded as an empirical question, and Krumhansl (1998) reports a study that makes an important start in this direction. Her aim was to assess the extent to which the topical structure of the Op. 132 movement (and the first movement of Mozart's C major String Quintet, K. 515—another of the works analyzed by Agawu) influenced listeners' continuous judgments of various attributes of the music. Krumhansl's listeners were Cornell University students with variable amounts of prior musical experience, but who were all far less expert in this specific music than are the authors of the analyses on which Krumhansl's study is based (Agawu, Allanbrook, Ratner). As an indicator, fewer than a third of her listeners recognized the Beethoven movement, and on average they spent less than an hour a week listening to classical music of any kind.

In separate tasks, and while listening to the music, these listeners made continuous judgments of the memorability, openness, and emotionality of the material that they heard. Krumhansl found that there was a reasonable degree of agreement between different listeners in their judgments of these three attributes over the course of the movement; that differences in the expertise of listeners had no significant effect on the pattern of judgments; and that listeners' ratings of the memorability, openness, and emotionality of the music were influenced by the presence or absence of the specific topics identified by Agawu. Krumhansl concludes that these results provide clear evidence for the psychological reality of Agawu's topics and that "their distinctive characteristics (such as tempo, rhythm, melodic figures) established them as psychological entities" (Krumhansl 1998: 132–133). She used this result to question the assumption made in the analytical literature that listeners need a high level of expertise to pick up the topical structure of classical music, but acknowledged that her study only provided evidence for listeners' abilities to detect the *presence* of topics, and could make no claims for the listeners' understanding of what Krumhansl called the connotations of those topics.

Krumhansl's experiment is important as a demonstration of the empirical reality of topics as part of a listening strategy and their role in organizing listeners' experiences of music. Nonetheless, the experiment can only demonstrate that listeners respond to the existence of "distinctive material" in the music in various ways, not how they perceive the meaning of that material—and a vital component of the concept of topic is the matter of topical *content*. It is one thing to accept that a reasonably broad spectrum of listeners, some with little familiarity with the specific musical style, will recognize the presence of distinctive material, but a rather different matter to claim that they will show any agreement about what that material means. In the absence of other empirical evidence[4] I will speculate about the general *kinds* of topics to which twenty-first century listeners to this music might be sensitive and consider how these might affect their experience of the music and its meaning.

Twenty-first Century Topics

Despite Krumhansl's demonstration of the psychological reality of topics, twenty-first century listeners must necessarily be very differently attuned to the topical world of the late eighteenth and early nineteenth centuries than were the listeners of that time. Even the most specialized expert listener who has attempted to reconstruct an early nineteenth century sensibility is in a situation that is utterly different from a true contemporary of Beethoven's—if only because of all the music that has sounded since then. A twenty-first century listener is inevitably not only deaf to some or many of the conventions that the music invokes, but also hears all kinds of later resonances that a contemporary of Beethoven's obviously could not. For example, I hear a "forward" reference to the quartets of Bartok and Shostakovich (and perhaps more generally to a kind of imprecise "Central European nationalism/folkism") in the bare and unharmonized motif in the viola and cello, imitated by the first and second violins, at bars 92–94 of the movement. One of the obvious consequences, therefore, of the 180 years that have elapsed since the quartet was first played is the erosion and loss of certain meanings, and the accumulation of others, by virtue of changes in both the musical and the more general environment that the piece inhabits.

But there is also a more fundamental cultural and perceptual change at work: from about the middle of the nineteenth century, there was a progressive but marked shift away from an Enlightenment aesthetic of sensibility and the play of social conventions and musical rhetoric, towards a much more serious, private, and individualistic aesthetic outlook, one which paradoxically embraced both more personalized ("artist as hero") and more universal ("eternal truths") perspectives (see Dahlhaus 1989; Goehr 1992). An intriguing aspect of Krumhansl's empirical study is that the responses of her late twentieth century listeners to the Mozart and Beethoven movements seemed partially to reflect this: she found that topics in the Mozart movement were perceived as defining the music's formal structure, while in Op. 132 "memorability was more strongly correlated with the amount of emotion, as if emotional emphasis is given to the memorable musical figures" (Krumhansl 1998: 133). As Dahlhaus (1989) and many others have pointed out, the change that took place between Enlightenment and Romantic sensibilities continues to play a significant role in the modern Western concert aesthetic. Attitudes to the classical canon retain a strongly late nineteenth century outlook, within which the idea of a "playful sensibility" and an engagement with rhetorical conventions plays a minor role by comparison with the belief that music articulates ineffable and timeless truths. The rapid and sometimes abrupt juxtaposition of topics that Agawu describes in Op. 132 might have been regarded as a challenging and witty play with the conventions of the time to a sophisticated 1825 listener. This same pattern of rapidly changing material might be heard by a present-day listener familiar with the music and culture of Viennese modernism as a striking portrayal by Beethoven of a crisis of identity—of the rapid and bewildering juxtaposition of different attributes of the self, with all the uncertainties that this reflects. This is certainly how McClary (2000: 119) interprets the movement, her analysis starting, "Few pieces offer so vivid an image of shattered subjectivity as the opening page of Op. 132." Equally, in the context of the nineteenth and twentieth century's increasing fascination with the personal lives and minds of creators, this theme of "bewildering uncertainty" might be attributed to Beethoven's own mental state. What is heard as virtuoso "play" with topical conventions from one perspective might be regarded as a profound portrayal of human subjectivity from another, or as the outpouring of Beethoven's own personal uncertainties from yet another.[5] As Subotnik, commenting on the consequences of historical distance, puts it: "The listener is . . . hearing overtones of intervening knowledge and experience which drown out or 'erase' various responses that could have originally been intended or anticipated, while adding others" (Subotnik 1988, reprinted in Scott 2000: 172).

The idea that the materials of the Op. 132 first movement, far from specifying a world of eighteenth century topics, might be heard as specifying a narrative of subjectivity (either in the abstract, or specifically Beethoven's) leads directly to one of the most widespread and powerful ideologies of listening—music as the expression or portrayal of emotions. Within this framework, the materials of music are claimed to specify abstracted and even essentialized emotions. In *The Language of Music* (Cooke 1959), for example, Cooke identifies a lexicon of musical expression types, whose emotional meaning is taken from the semantic content of the words which the music sets or some other clearly semantic context (such as the place of the music in the narrative of the mass). Cooke argues that the harmonic series is a powerful factor in determining the emotional meaning of each of the musical archetypes that he identifies, but he also acknowledges the role of "conventions of use" in refining or helping to establish the meaning of the expression types, and in this respect the theory is not far removed from a theory of emotional "topics." One difference is that for Agawu, and particularly for Monelle, topics are much more culturally embedded and ramified than are Cooke's emotion terms: they are manifest in a highly elaborated network of literary, pictorial, poetic, philosophical, and enacted forms. For example, in discussing various ways in which music makes use of "galloping" or "horses' hooves" materials, Monelle (2000) proposes that there are a number of differentiated equestrian topics that are also demonstrated in contemporary literature, iconography, and social practice. These topics demarcate important distinctions between the various cultural positions which equestrian activity (hunting, travel, military) has occupied over history, reflecting and helping to construct the cultural significance that the horse as a cultural unit played.

But although Cooke presents his emotion terms in rather a bald and narrow fashion, a more elaborated view that addresses the emotions in a manner that is much closer to that of topic theory is perfectly possible. Contemporary culture is full of representations of the emotions (in film, drama, painting, sculpture, literature—as well as music), and the idea that the meaning of music is more or less synonymous with the expression of emotions is probably the most widespread assumption among listeners in contemporary culture. In the liner notes that accompany the Lindsay String Quartet's 1987 recording of the Op. 132 quartet, for example, Peter Cropper (the leader of the quartet) writes: "I have felt for a long time that for a listener to get inside these late string quartets, he must try to delve into Beethoven's innermost thoughts. . . . What Beethoven has to say about life in this music cannot be described in words. However, there are many words and indications that he himself wrote in the score to help the performers realise his feelings and, if we can understand these markings, then we are nearer to getting into Beethoven's mind." Music is portrayed here and in a great deal of other writing as a seismograph of subjectivity, conveying and expressing innermost thoughts and feelings with an abstractness that guarantees its truth and purity, but also renders it untranslatable.

In summary, the idea of relatively distinct and culturally elaborated topics of the kind discussed by Agawu, Allanbrook, and Monelle is displaced in much of the twentieth century discourse on listening by the idea that music is primarily concerned with the expression of emotions, and that specific emotions are conveyed, or triggered, by particular musical procedures. These range from rather general features of the musical material, such as major/minor mode distinctions, or types of harmonic progression (cf. Sloboda 1991), to the more specific "lexicons" of musical gesture, such as Clynes's suggestion (Clynes 1977) that music makes use of what he calls "sentic types"—particular expressions of emotion encoded by means of their melodic/rhythmic shape. These sentic types are rather like "emotional topics," based largely on the kinematic/dynamic qualities of the music. The dramatic rise in the influence of psychology as an explanatory framework within the twentieth century has had the consequence that it is now common for emotions to be presented as being founded on psychological, or even biological, principles with a high degree of cross-cultural and transhistorical constancy. A strongly essentialist psychological account has displaced the manifest conventions of an approach based on rhetoric—a narrative of personal and subjective emotions as opposed to a play of social conventions (cf. Cook and Dibben 2001).

As an illustration, consider just the first 21 bars of the movement. A listener might hear a sequence of emotional "topics," specified by invariant properties, which would go something like this:

1. After an indeterminate start (see below), the first eight bars are heard as a "questing and tragic spirituality."

The invariants that specify this include the minor mode (tragic), the motet-like homophony (religious/spiritual by association; calm and patient by virtue of tempo and pitch profile), and the registral expansion (seeking/exploring) and uncadenced ending (unended quest).

2. At bars 9–10, a new emotional topic appears: "anxious and frenetic uncertainty." The invariants are the diminished seventh harmony (anxiety, uncertainty), the rhythmic rapidity (frenetic), the loud dynamic (aroused), and the overall pitch contour that moves down only to return to its starting point (ineffectual).

3. Bars 11–17 are heard as "cautious, but increasingly resolute, determination," and the invariants are: thin texture becoming thicker, quiet dynamic becoming louder, and increasing metrical clarity (all of these specifying caution becoming increasingly confident/determined); minor mode (tragic); appoggiaturas (sorrowful); rising pitch profile and increasing rhythmic activity (increasing hope and determination).

4. Bars 18–20 are heard as "anxiety, leading to collapse, followed by determined restoration," and the invariants are: increasing amounts of uneven rhythmic activity (rising anxiety); convergence to unison rhythm and pitch (sudden loss of direction, uncertainty); descending pitch contour (loss of hope); re-emergence of harmony out of unison (restoration); clear voice-leading and even rhythm (determination).

Structural Process

Topics—rhetorical or emotional—are not the only way in which the movement is organized. Agawu identifies tonal/harmonic process, organized around the framework of a beginning–middle–end paradigm, as the structural principle that not only ensures the unity and integrity of this and the other works that he analyzes, but also constitutes the counter-pole to topical organization in the semiotic interplay between rhetoric and structure. I too want to consider what happens structurally in this movement, but from a more directly perceptual perspective than the Schenkerian approach that Agawu uses, and paying rather more explicit attention to dimensions other than tonality—such as rhythm, register, texture, and dynamics.

First, consider the details of the very opening of the movement (example 6.1). The unaccompanied, *pianissimo* G#2 minim on the cello with which the work starts is highly indeterminate, and with no other context, a listener can have no idea of what kind of tonal or rhythmic event this sound specifies, though this becomes clearer when the G#2 rises to A2. Rhythmically there is still little that a listener can perceive (two attack points specify a time interval but nothing more), but harmonically there is a strong tendency to hear the rise of semitone as a move from tension to resolution on the basis of the widespread style convention that could be called "generalized appoggiatura": dissonances on strong beats tend to move by semitone or tone step (up or down) to consonances on weak beats.

The second bar clarifies the perceptual indeterminacy of the first in a number of ways. At the beginning of the bar the viola joins the cello, followed halfway through that bar by the second violin, so that two-part and then three-part harmony replaces the harmonic indeterminacy of the first bar's monody. Second, the regular minims, coupled with a repetition in the second bar of the dissonance/consonance (or tense/relaxed) alternation in the first, specify duple meter. Third, the harmonic events of bar 2 (harmonic tension resolving onto a major triad [E major] whose root is a fifth above the corresponding single pitch [A] in the first bar) dramatically narrow the range of tonal events that the sounds of these first two bars specify—really to just one: the dominant of a minor key. The remainder of the opening eight-bar passage confirms and intensifies these elements, the entry of the first violin in bar 3 thickening the texture and continuing the slow upward expansion of the register. Each bar replicates the pattern of a tense and dissonant first half resolving onto a stable and consonant second half, within a very narrow harmonic field, but with an expanding registral compass—from a single note at the start to a range of nearly four octaves at the start of bar 6. The first seven bars maintain an unbroken succession of minims at slow tempo, but the crotchet movement and change of harmony on every beat in bar 8 break these rhythmic and harmonic patterns and join with the crescendo at the end of the bar to push forward to the *forte* and *Allegro* material of bar 9.

In summary, by the downbeat of bar 9 a listener will have heard a trajectory from almost total rhythmic and harmonic indeterminacy at the start, to the consolidation of a minor key with a strong emphasis on its dominant harmony; slow duple meter articulated by regular minims with a strict alternation of harmonic tension and release; and a process of registral expansion from a narrow region centred around middle C at bar 3 to a point of maximum compass at bar 8—a process that starts to turn in on itself just as this eight-bar passage comes to an end. There is a pervasive sense of repetition in the fixed pattern of minim movement and harmonic alternation, but otherwise the material is relatively undifferentiated—though the motivic pattern of the four minims in the cello in bars 1–2 is clearly repeated in a transposed form in the first violin in bars 3 and 4.[6]

Bar 9 brings the first of the many abrupt changes of material that are a striking feature of this movement. Bar 8 breaks the established harmonic pattern, with the result that bar 9 simply prolongs the unstable and tense harmony (a diminished seventh) with which bar 8 finishes. More strikingly, the tempo, texture, dynamic and motivic characteristics heard so far are all swept away by the arrival of the three lower instruments on a *forte* staccato crotchet and then silence. Above this, the first violin plays a rapid figuration, ending up—after an equally sudden diminuendo—on a mirroring *piano* staccato chord in the lower instruments, with the first violin on an appoggiatura that resolves just as the chord falls silent (example

6.1). With the resolution note restated and held in the first violin, the cello starts with new material again—a conjunct melody with a prominent dotted rhythm in a high register. As the inner parts fill out the initially bare texture, the first violin takes over the continuation and development of the cello's material, and with stable harmony and texture the music adopts a much more predictable pattern. The stability lasts for little more than five bars, however; the four instruments one by one collapse into a pitch and rhythmic unison[7] that equally abruptly opens back out into crotchet chords in four and five part harmony—before a sudden return to quiet, slow music (sustained chords in the lower instruments, an arpeggiated melody in the first violin), and a resumption of the whole kaleidoscopic process.

What this blow-by-blow account of the first 21 bars is intended to convey is the rapid juxtaposition of abruptly different materials—not only the topics, but also the manner in which they are presented, and the contrasts of dynamic, texture, and register. At the same time, however, there are at least two invariant features of the music that hold it together. One is the strong instrumental identity and coherence of the ensemble: the sounds of a string quartet on the one hand have the capacity to specify the individual identity of the four instruments, and on the other hand have a very high level of blend by virtue of the physical similarity of the instruments and of the actions required to produce sound, so much so that they can at times appear to specify a single "multi-instrument." The other invariant is the stable harmonic coherence of the passage: with the exception of the brief unison dive to the flat supertonic ($B\flat$) in bar 19, the whole of this opening passage revolves around tonic and dominant harmony.[8]

What are the structural events, then, that this passage establishes, and how does it do so? The first eight bars establish the following principal characteristics:

- The invariance of the instrumental group (through timbral commonality).

- The duple meter (through the regular alternation of consonance and dissonance, changes of register, and motivic parallelisms).
- The harmonic framework (through the use of a very limited range of harmonies—almost entirely tonic and dominant).
- The regular binary phrase structure (through registral, dynamic, and textural changes).
- The slow tempo (through long inter-onset intervals).

At bar 9, many of these are cast into doubt or dissolved:

- The tempo changes abruptly—though it is at first difficult to determine the tempo of the music at all, since the rapid first violin part, though "fast" in a literal sense, can also be heard as highly embellished but slow.[9]
- The sense of meter is dissolved for two reasons. First, the melodic contour of the violin part simply repeats at crotchet intervals, and provides no information about how these crotchet units might be organized together; and because the break in this pattern in the middle of bar 10 (first into pure rising arpeggiation, and then a pair of quavers) is hard to interpret, the undifferentiated arpeggio is metrically ambiguous. Furthermore, the pair of quavers in bar 10 sound like a resolution of the harmonic dissonance in bars 9 and 10—but falling on the weakest beat of the bar, suddenly quiet, and too brief to be convincing, they not only fail to achieve harmonic resolution but also contribute to the sense of metrical uncertainty.
- The motivic structure is dissolved, since the first violin part simply consists of more or less embellished arpeggiation.
- The harmony is destabilized (through the use of only diminished harmony).
- The established dynamic context is disrupted by the sudden *forte* at bar 9, which rapidly, and with a sense of arbitrariness about it, returns in bar 10 to the initial *piano*.

At bar 11, however, an integration and stability begins of a kind not yet heard in the piece: a simple and distinct dotted motif is heard in the cello, directly imitated by the first violin two bars later, and then developed with many of its rhythmic features preserved (first violin bars 15–18, viola bar 16, second violin bar 17–18) at periods that confirm the music's duple meter. This imitation, which helps to establish or confirm the meter, also serves in the end to de-stabilize it: the rate of repetition gets faster in bars 17 and 18 so that by bar 19 the music has degenerated into undifferentiated dotted rhythm. The homophonic crotchets of bar 20, broken only by the pair of quavers in the first violin on the last beat, lead back to the slow, quiet music of bar 21 (motivically, harmonically, and texturally associated with the music that starts the movement)—at which point a more compressed version of the process starts again.

These features of the opening 21 bars amount to three different kinds of music—and constitute three different attempts to start the piece. The first attempt is the eight-bar motet-like passage that has already been described. This is not only literally the start of the piece, but in purely temporal terms is also a substantial chunk of music—40 seconds solidly rooted in A minor. As is often the case with this kind of texture, the music is both abstractly harmonic (a succession of homophonic chords) and also residually motivic: the basic shape of the four-note motif in the cello is not only an invariant feature of these eight bars, but also appears in more or less altered forms throughout this movement and in other parts of the quartet as a whole—most obviously in the third movement.

The second "start" is at bar 9, where the first violin suddenly breaks out into much more active and brilliant music. The silence of the other three instruments after their intial punctuating chord somewhat undermines the capacity of this music to function as stable and "declarative" material—and really it sounds more like a rather rhetorical *response* to something than a *statement* of anything. For a moment, though, and following on from the serious motet of the first eight bars, I can hear this as the movement starting, after a slow introduction; then, within a matter of seconds (no more than five or six on a recording by the Borodin String Quartet[10]), it has faded and disappeared.

The third "start" begins hesitantly at bar 11 as an inconspicuous melody on the cello against the sustained note on which the first violin's cadenza-like material comes to rest. But as the other instruments join in, and the melody moves around the ensemble, it gathers intensity and texture and, through imitation of the dotted head rhythm, assumes a kind of definiteness and distinction (the identity of affirmation, derived from imitation) that makes it a real contender as declarative material. Once again, however, the material dissolves—this time through the imitative collapse in bars 18–19, and the music returns to abbreviated forms of the slow (bar 21) and cadenza-like (bar 22) materials that have already been heard. With no single, convincing beginning, the music starts—prematurely, it seems, and with a strange kind of boot-strapping tactic—to refer back to itself as *if* it were already well established. Three "failed" starts leave a sense that after a minute of music, and a lot of different kinds of material, the piece has still not established itself.

Texture and Motion

Musical texture has been discussed only sporadically in the analytical or perceptual literature, exceptions being Berry (1976), Levy (1982), Drabkin (1985), and Sutcliffe (1987; 2003). The textures, and frequent *changes* of texture, in this movement are a striking and perceptually salient characteristic of the music, and provide the basis for my last account of what there is to hear in this piece. The opening starts with the thinnest and barest of textures: a single instrument playing single notes. There is a minimal thickening at bar 2 when the viola enters a major third above the cello, and again in the second half of the bar with the entry of the second violin. At the entry of the first violin in bar 3, the cello drops out, and it is not until the start of bar 5 that the full four-voiced texture of the quartet is first heard. By this point, the registral expansion discussed earlier has begun, reaching a maximum at the start of bar 7, the four instruments evenly spaced at intervals of a minor tenth. Texture is a function of both the registral space and the number of elements that fill it—so that the narrowly focused and comparatively dense texture at the start of bar 3 (three instruments within the span of a tritone) is progressively stretched open to reach the dramatically wider and sparser texture at bar 7 (four instruments within a span of nearly four octaves). At this point, the textural-registral process turns back on itself and begins to contract, fill and accelerate, reaching the reiterated six-note chord with a span of two and a half octaves that leads into the Allegro at bar 9.

This "micro analysis" of texture deals with a process that occupies little more than 40 seconds of music, but which constitutes a compelling perceptual attribute of the movement's opening, seeming somehow to flex the muscles of the rather subdued material with which the quartet begins. That "flexing" results in the sudden outburst at bar 9, bringing with it an utterly different kind of texture. After the chord on the downbeat of bar 9, the changing vertical densities of bars 1–8 are replaced by the rapid linear activity of the first violin, and then by various mixtures of linearity and simultaneity in the passage from bar 11 back to the purely chordal—but much more mobile—texture of bar 20.

One of the obvious perceptual consequences of textural difference is an apparent change of volume (in the spatial sense). As a first approximation, textures with widely spaced elements are perceived as occupying a larger volume than those with narrowly spaced elements. I hear this very clearly in the opening eight bars, where the opening single pitch is "multiplied" by successive entries that then diverge. My perception of the opening up of some kind of virtual space can be explained in terms of the auditory streaming principles that Bregman (1990) discusses extensively: the four instruments of the quartet are identifiable as separate streams (by virtue of timbre, register, and differences in vibrato), and as a consequence are perceived as four sources occupying distinct locations,

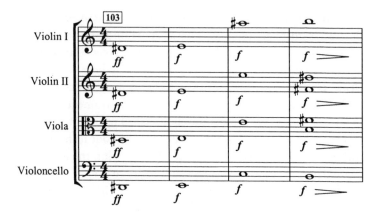

Example 6.2 Bars 103–106 of the First Movement of Beethoven's String
Quartet in A minor, Op. 132.

which thus define some kind of space. A dramatic illustration of
this is heard later in the movement at bars 103–106 (see figure 6.2):
in bars 103 and 104 all four instruments play semibreves (occupying
the whole bar) in unison and octave doublings, but at 105—still
in semibreves—the four instruments break out into four-part harmony, and then (with double stopping) six-part harmony at 106.
The effect is of a narrow space, or a singularity, bursting open.

The size of the space, however, is not the only consideration.
There is also the matter of how that space is occupied, and here I
return to the questions of motion and agency that were discussed
in chapter 3. As the examples in that chapter illustrated, virtual
motion is specified by a number of different properties of sound,
among them rhythm (rate and manner of motion), dynamic
(approach, withdrawal), pitch (direction) and articulation (weight,
force); and agency is experienced as either subjective identification
(motion experienced as self-motion) or the actions of other agents
(motion experienced as the motion of others)—or as a hybrid state
that combines both "subjective" and "objective" components.

Using these principles I will consider the changing perception of virtual motion, and of agency, again over just the first 21 bars of the movement.

In terms of motion and agency, the opening is uncertain, as the movement is in so many other respects. The homophonic texture and slow and even rhythm seem to specify slow, coordinated, and directed motion (directed because of the functional harmony and largely predictable voice-leading)—and therefore some kind of self motion, perhaps similar to the coordinated movement of the parts of a single body that I described for the Mozart Quintet passage in chapter 3. But this is only when the passage has got going—by about bar 3 or 4: the very beginning is uncertain because the successive instrumental entries, identifiable by timbre (cello, viola, violin) as well as register, seem on the one hand to specify separate agents, but on the other hand are so timbrally blended, and close in register, as to appear to grow out of one another. The eight-bar passage gives the impression of building a single entity out of separate agents/components. That entity is on the one hand the real entity of the string quartet, and on the other a virtual object that I hear as having a bodily character. This body on the one hand has the quality of a body separate from myself, because I have heard its assembly out of separate parts; and on the other hand it behaves as if it is *my* body due to the coordinated way in which the four parts flex themselves around the central listening position that I seem to occupy. This "body" expands to bar 7, and then draws back in on itself before the sudden change that takes place at bar 9.

Bars 9 and 10 are really a ballistic trajectory launched with a bit of a bang (the chord in the lower instruments) and just about held with a slightly hesitant "catch" (the quieter and metrically floating chord in the lower instruments on the last beat of bar 10). The rapid motion of this sudden outburst is self-evident, but I also hear overall immobility across the two bars (due to the static harmony—until the catch), as if something or someone is flapping about on the spot. What or who do I hear moving here? The singularity of the line affords hearing this as self motion, but actually I hear this more as the motion of something or someone else—perhaps because of its sudden contrast to the much more measured motion that precedes it, and with which I feel a stronger identification.

After the "catch" in A minor at the end of bar 10, a predominantly linear texture ensues—but utterly different from the linearity that precedes it. First, even though the tempo is the same, it is both much slower in that it doesn't "flap about," and also much more purposeful in that it actually seems to go somewhere. Although this is the first appearance of dotted rhythms, the overall sense is of rather smooth and predictable motion. There is an uncertainty at first about where the line in this linear texture really is (in the active cello, or the first violin left floating on a stationary but prominent E_5 after its burst of activity?), but this is resolved by bar 13. The texture here consists of a compellingly conjunct line with homophonic support, with the result that I hear this largely as myself moving forward[11]—a little hesitantly to begin with, but then with increasing clarity and sense of purpose. But the solid support soon starts to become more polyphonic and active—to generate offshoots of itself/myself—and its/my actions become more anxious and undirected as I get/it gets crowded and engulfed by those other bits and pieces (bars 18–19). Pulled jerkily (dotted-rhythmically) down into a low and narrow place at the start of bar 20 (three unisons doubled at the octave below), I then escape or emerge (and there is a sense that this is both me and someone/something else) through more than two octaves of textural space, with powerful and then suddenly calmer actions, to more or less the same place (around bar 7) where I was less than a minute ago.

In just over a minute of music, I hear a complex succession of textures that specify different kinds of motion, different conditions of agency (degrees of self/other), and different kinds of multiplicity (individual, group, parts of a whole). Mixed in with this *virtual* motion and agency, I also perceive something of the real physicality, and agency, of the four actual instrumentalists, as well as engaging with the music in something like its own "music-material" terms. While I experience a rapid succession of identities and kinds of motion, I am also aware of an environment of musical events within the work—of statements, motifs, repetitions, harmonic tensions, phrases, and so on. The autonomous character of music is *not* entirely illusory, but it is also only one aspect of what I experience in music—and surely that is what listening to music is like. At times music does have the power—or rather the specific kinds of features—to draw a listener into a virtual reality consisting of objects and events that are experienced simultaneously as motifs, rhythmic groups, and cadences, as well as spaces, actions, places, and agents. And at other times it remains firmly anchored in the everyday world through the real actions, objects, ideologies, words, and social functions with which it is entwined.

Summary

The detailed discussion of this Beethoven quartet movement has shown that a number of different ways of hearing the music, or a number of different components of a composite hearing, can be tackled from an ecological perspective. The music is an example of "absolute and autonomous music," and some attributes of the perceptual analysis presented here are consistent with that outlook—most obviously the structural processes which set the music going, and which are used to make uncertain its own formal procedures: the ambiguity about really where and how it starts.[12] But much more of what emerges from this analysis lies outside the framework of autonomy: the rhetorical and emotional topics, the sense of virtual motion and agency, the perception of physical action. This supposedly autonomous music is only residually (or at best partially) so from a perceptual point of view; the world into which listeners are drawn does not consist simply of the music's own formal processes, but is far more heterogeneous and heteronomous.

As I recognized at the start of the chapter, my analysis makes no attempt (and can make no attempt) to indicate which if any of the perceptual opportunities that I have described might dominate in the experience of an individual listener. On the basis of what I hear, and using the analyses of this movement by others as indicators of what they hear,[13] the supposed autonomy of this music is as perceptually illusory as it is theoretically unsustainable. Nonetheless, the "world of the work" does constitute a particular kind of environment, and one into which listeners can be powerfully drawn. One of the remarkable characteristics of our perceptual systems, and of the adaptability of human consciousness, is the ability to change the focus, and what might be called the "scale of focus," of attention—from great breadth and diversity of awareness to the sense of being absorbed in a singularity. At one moment I can be aware of the people, clothing, furniture, coughing, shuffling, air conditioning and lighting of a performance venue, among which are the sounds and sights of a performance of Beethoven's string quartet Op. 132 and all that those sounds specify; and at another moment I am aware of nothing at all beyond a visceral engagement with musical events of absorbing immediacy and compulsion. The transition between these different perceptual worlds, or the interruption of one by another, can be disturbing and disruptive (when the ticking of a neighbor's watch breaks into the environment of Op. 132, for instance). Yet a whole ideology of submissive listening, asserting the special power of classical music, has encouraged what is at times a fanatically protective attitude to the "world of the work." Music does afford intensely absorbing and particular kinds of perceptual meanings, and it is therefore not surprising that the idea of autonomy and its associated listening practices has its staunch defenders and has acquired powerful cultural prestige. It is nonetheless just one among many ways of listening.

Conclusion

To listen to music is to engage with music's meaning. As the preceding chapters have shown, an ecological approach to listening provides a basis on which to understand the perceptual character of musical meaning. Perception is fundamentally concerned with picking up what is happening in the world, and picking up what is happening in music is central to musical meaning—if the phrase is understood in an appropriately inclusive manner. A number of authors (Balzano, Dowling and Harwood, Leman) have shown how ecological principles can account for the way in which listeners perceive structural processes in music, but in a more far-reaching manner people also listen to the ways in which musical sounds specify the wider world of which they are a part. As the analyses in this book have demonstrated in music ranging from Mozart and Beethoven to Hendrix, Zappa, and Fatboy Slim, the sounds of music specify a huge diversity of sources:[1] the instruments and recording media from which they emanate, the musical styles to which they belong, the social functions in which they participate, the emotional states and bodily actions of their performers, the spaces and places—virtual and real—which they inhabit, the discourses with which they are intertwined. Because instruments, bodies, loudspeakers, stages, cathedrals, and clubs are palpably physical, there is little difficulty in accepting them as sources that are specified in sound. I hear the sound *of* a drum kit, *of* flutter-tonguing, *of* a club as I pass its doorway. But there has been more resistance to the idea that cultures, social practices, emotional states, and ideological allegiances could be conceived as "sources" because they have been regarded as too abstract, too nonmaterial. This is unnecessarily restrictive: cultures, emotions, and ideologies are not *only* material, but they are all necessarily manifest in material forms of one sort or another, among which there are the sounds of those phenomena. Vienna around 1900, or 1960s American youth culture, or the 1990s British clubbing scene are all cultures and subcultures that are manifest in material forms (images, buildings, language, clothing) to which perceivers can be more or less attuned—and musical sounds are one of those material forms. These cultures and subcultures (and instruments, bodies, emotions, social practices) are the *sources* of those sounds, since they constitute the conditions and circumstances that gave rise to the music. In the same way, a cadence in A minor, a dominant prolongation, or a gavotte rhythm can be regarded as the (structural) sources of a sound that a listener hears.

The structuralist orientation of traditional music analysis and the psychology of music has meant that both disciplines have tended to confine themselves to a consideration of the immediate sources that lie either within an individual work or a generic style. In this respect, both traditions lean toward an autonomous view of music. By contrast, an ecological perspective addresses both immanent properties in music and also a far wider and more diverse range of other sources—without abandoning a commitment to the material manner in which these sources are specified. While cognitive and semiotic accounts tend towards abstraction, giving a central role to explicit mental representations in the explanation of "higher level" phenomena, the ecological approach challenges the idea of representation in perception and resists ordering phenomena hierarchically: levels play little or no role in what I have presented in this book. Ecological theory focuses instead on the particular invariants—perhaps distributed over different time spans, but not differing in abstraction—that specify different sources. It may require a longer stretch of music for someone to perceive that it is the Borodin String Quartet playing than to perceive that there is a cello being played, but that does not imply a difference of level or abstraction. It may simply be that the invariants that specify the Borodin String Quartet are not present at the start of the sound, or are distributed over a longer period.[2] In fact, as I observed in chapter 2, so-called high-level properties of music often seem to be identified extremely quickly: the recording of Hendrix's "Star Spangled Banner" demonstrates that the Woodstock audience perceived the identity of their national anthem, and seemed to hear the critical irony of Hendrix playing it in those particular circumstances, after just two notes had been played. Central to the approach adopted in this book, therefore, is the need to pay careful attention to the manner in which musical meanings (sources) are specified in sound and to consider what the invariants for those meanings (sources) might be.

It is important to reiterate that this does not imply any kind of determinacy in the perception of musical meaning—for two reasons. First, invariants will often specify more than one source, and in music—as the discussions of all the examples in this book have shown—the multiplicity of such sources is often overwhelming. Second, the mutualism of perceiver and environment means that different perceivers will be attuned to different invariants and at different times. We all have the potential to hear different things in the same music—but the fact that we don't (or at least not all the time) is an indication of the degree to which we share a common environment, and experience common perceptual learning or adaptation. This commonality is only partial, and the explicit mutualism that the ecological approach espouses emphasizes a theme that has surfaced at various points throughout this book: if the principle of mutualism means that listening must be considered in relation to the needs and capacities of *particular* listeners, rather than in general or abstracted terms, then whose listening is this book about?

Whose Listening?

There are various responses to this question and the challenge that it presents. The most obvious is that the book is primarily about my own listening, as I have made explicit at various points in the preceding chapters. Since the purpose of the observations and analyses in this book is to try to explain the general processes involved in perceiving musical meaning, there is no particular significance in whose listenings these are: they are simply my raw material. Second, though the listenings that are recorded in this book may be idiosyncratic in certain respects, they can be considered approximately representative of a wider category of listeners that I represent: listeners enculturated in Western traditions with formal music training. Third, as in the analysis of the Beethoven quartet movement, an attempt can be made partially to bracket the particularity of the listener and to try to enumerate a number of co-existent and equally "available" attributes that are specified in musical sound without trying to prescribe which ones are actually heard by any particular listeners or categories of listener.

As discussed earlier in this book, a different approach, and one that has not been attempted here, would be to gather empirical evidence about what it is that larger numbers of different listeners *actually* hear. Despite the rapid growth of the psychology of music over the last 25 years or so, this evidence is still surprisingly hard to find. A considerable amount of empirical research has tried to take into account possible differences between listeners with different degrees of formal musical training, but these differences have usually been considered in the context of highly focused research questions (such as listeners' judgments of the appropriateness of a specific note in a tonal context, or the position of a section boundary in a piece of music), and in relation to a narrow spectrum of listener types (typically university students with different amounts of musical training). More open-ended and wide-ranging studies are rare or almost entirely absent, perhaps for a mixture of reasons. One is that it is very hard to do this kind of study in an effective manner. The intuitively appealing idea of getting a diverse group of individuals, playing them a selection of music examples (perhaps taken from a wide spectrum of musical styles) and asking them to write down or say what they hear, is fraught with problems: the potential arbitrariness in choosing musical examples; differences in people's capacity to express in language what they hear; the inaccessibility of unconscious components of listening; the impact of the more or less artificial situation on people's usual listening habits; their own assumptions about what they imagine they "should" be hearing and writing about; and so on. The absence of such studies can also be attributed to a widespread assumption within the psychology of music that the perception and interpretation of musical *structures* should be the central focus of listening research, and that, while listeners may differ in their discrimination of such structures, or the explicitness with which they can report them or make judgments about them, the processes and representations which are involved are fundamentally the same. Some of the most influential work in the psychology of music has adopted this perspective[3] and as a result the question of what different kinds of listeners actually hear, or how they use music, has been sidelined as a more sociological issue that has only recently been tackled in publications such as DeNora's *Music in Everyday Life* (DeNora 2000), or the exploratory study by Sloboda, O'Neill, and Ivaldi (2001).

The approach adopted in this book is therefore something of a compromise. There simply is not the empirical evidence on which to base a discussion of listening that would take account of all the different ways in which people listen and the different phenomena that they hear. And in fact if such empirical evidence did exist, any theoretical thread that attempted to join it all together would be swamped by the overwhelming weight and diversity of "evidence."

So this is not a book that summarizes, or tries to make sense of, a body of pre-existing empirical data—and in that sense it is predominantly not an empirical book. But neither does it aim to be abstractly theoretical; my own listening and responses to music were my underlying motivation for attempting such a book in the first place and are inevitably the basis of my descriptions and interpretations of specific musical phenomena. My approach has been to suggest or claim that certain kinds of things are heard in music; at times to enumerate a number of different ways in which people might attend to the same sounds, but never to assert that this is how everyone will always hear these sounds; and wherever possible to try to explain in reasonably systematic terms why and how those attributes are heard.

It is a truism that different people perceive notionally the same event in different ways and on different occasions—but the starting point for this book is a belief that these individual differences are the specific manifestations of the same general principles of perception. What I have done is to use my own perception, and the formal and informal perceptions of others (the things that people say and write about what they hear in music), as a basis from which to discuss those general principles, strongly guided by the more general ecological theory presented in the introduction. To the question, "Whose listening?" my answer is therefore, "Mine more than anyone else's," but with the generalisability that comes from the attempt to analyze and explain what I hear in terms of general perceptual theory.

The Psychology of Music

The great majority of work in the psychology of music has adopted a cognitivist approach that is fundamentally different from the outlook presented in this book. Ecological theory differs from "mainstream" psychology of music in a number of ways: in emphasizing the mutualism of organism and environment, it offers an alternative to the mentalism of the cognitive tradition; it adopts a more embodied outlook through the central relationship between perception and action; it resists the idea that perception should be understood in terms of internal representations; and it eschews rigid adherence to hierarchical structures and processing stages. Ecological writing has also been critical of some of the empirical methods that the cognitive tradition has typically employed. Caricaturing somewhat, these methods tend to feature simplified materials abstracted from their familiar contexts; artificial tasks employing unusual and constrained "responses" from participants; and a lack of active engagement between participant and material. The drawbacks of using highly abstracted materials have become much more generally recognized within the psychology of music (see, e.g., Dowling 1989 for a commentary), and an increasing volume of research has become far more aware of the case for "ecological validity"—the need for experimental situations, tasks, and materials to be realistic. This means both trying to use procedures that have at least some similarity to actual musical practices and using appropriate materials. But making a decision about experimental materials depends on having some notion of how musical materials might be appropriately described, and one of the aims of an ecological approach is to find ecologically appropriate descriptions of events—in this case musical events.

The influence and prestige of the physical sciences mean that it is all too easy to assume that standard acoustical descriptions of sounds are the appropriate ones to use in psychological research—endorsed by the accuracy and technological sophistication of the instruments from which they are often derived. But an important distinction needs to be drawn between two kinds of acoustics: physical acoustics and ecological acoustics. The spectrum photographs of passages of music shown in Cogan (1984), for instance, are concerned with physical acoustics. They illustrate physical facts about musical sounds and can make no claims about the relevance of what is shown for a human listener. Imagine a spectrum photo with a fascinating and highly structured pattern of activity in a frequency range that is beyond the limits of human hearing. The photo is not a false representation of the stimulus, but it has no relevance for human listeners. Ecological acoustics, by contrast, is the attempt to describe the properties of stimulus information in terms that are relevant to the perceptual capacities of the organism in question—a matter that is clearly species specific. Gibson pointed out that phenomena can be described at scales ranging from the subatomic to the cosmic, but that "the appropriate scale for animals is the intermediate one of millimeters to kilometers, and it is appropriate because the world and the animal are then comparable" (Gibson 1966: 22). The general principle of ecological scale is an important corrective to the temptation to believe that properties of perceptual objects must be significant simply because they can be shown to be there by a measuring device.

Deciding what the "appropriate" scale might be for any organism (and in any specific perceptual domain) is not straightforward, since it cannot simply be assumed that phenomena at some particular scale are irrelevant on the basis of a superficial impression of an organism's sensory capacities. As the only directly observable aspect of the human auditory system, the external ear is little more than a rather simple, fleshy object—from which it might be concluded that audition is rather a crude sense. But first appearances can be deceptive, and the auditory system is actually sensitive to astonishingly tiny variations in amplitude and frequency. What is needed is a systematic investigation of the stimulus properties that directly inform musical behavior, by analogy with Gibson's (and other ecological psychologists') investigations of the properties of the visual world that inform the successful coordination of perception and action (as, for example, in catching a ball). There is already a body of work within the psychology of music that has made important progress in this direction: some examples are Balzano's (1982; 1987) work on the set-theoretic attributes of pitch-class collections, and their tonality-specifying properties; Butler's related work on "rare" intervals and tonality (e.g. Butler 1989); Parncutt's psychoacoustical approach to tonal harmony (Parncutt

1989); Large's research on synchronizing with temporal sequences (e.g. Large and Palmer 2002); and my own research on rhythm perception (Clarke 1987).

Empirical Questions

One consequence of adopting an ecological approach is the need to reassess the terminology that is habitually used to describe music from the perspective of a listener, and the assumptions about listening that come with that terminology. As others have pointed out (e.g. Serafine 1988; Cook 1994), empirical work in the psychology of music has tended rather uncritically to assume the psychological reality of musical entities (such as the note, for example) which may be derived from particular notational and analytical practices. That notation in turn may reflect the preoccupations or needs of composers and performers, but not the experiences of listeners.

In a similar manner, at the start of an essay concerned with ecological acoustics, Gaver (1993b) presents the following scenario:

Imagine that you are a participant in a psychology experiment on the perception of complex sounds. Your task is to listen to a series of sounds and write down a brief description of what you hear.

"A single-engine propeller plane flying past," you write in response to the first sound, pleased with yourself for providing so much detail.

The experimenter, on the other hand, is not pleased. He says, with some irritation, "No, no, no. Write down what you *hear*, not what you think it is."

"But I heard a propeller plane fly past," you object. "I didn't think about it; that's what I heard."

"You may not have thought about it consciously," he retorts, "but you didn't hear an airplane, you heard a quasi-harmonic tone lasting approximately 3 seconds with smooth variations in the fundamental frequency and the overall amplitude. That's what I want you to tell me about."

"I don't understand you," you persist, though a little hesitantly. "I didn't hear whatever it is you said. I heard a propeller plane."

The experimenter sighs and explains patiently, "No, you *interpreted* the sound as a propeller plane by matching the incoming stimulus with representations stored in memory. I'm not interested in how people interpret sounds; that's a job for cognitive science. I'm interested in how you hear the sound itself. Now try again . . ." (Gaver 1993b: 285–286)

The dialogue can be seen as a lesson in acoustical versus eco- logical terminology—and here the connection with more conven- tionally musical sounds is important. The descriptions of what untrained listeners hear can sometimes get treated with the same exasperation as in Gaver's dialogue, as if their failure to use the con- ventional technical language is attributed to incompetence or an excess of "subjective interpretation." A different view (illustrated in Dibben 2001, and in somewhat different terms in DeNora 2000) is to regard these descriptions as the basis for a broader ecological description of music, and the basis for an ecological musical acous- tics. If people commonly describe certain kinds of musical sounds as "soap opera music," "Euro pop"—or "Sturm und Drang," for that matter—then this provides the starting point for an explora- tion of the invariants that specify each of those sources.

Along similar lines, the ideas about motion and agency in music raised in chapter 3 suggest an investigation of the terminology that people use to describe these kinds of perceptions[4] and of the invari- ants that specify different kinds of perceived motion in music. In particular, it might be possible to determine whether the distinc- tion between self-motion and the motion of others is borne out empirically, and, if so, whether there are specific stimulus features that can be identified as the invariants for self-motion. I suggested in chapter 3 that the distinction between unified and coordinated parts on the one hand, and un-coordinated and independent parts on the other, may relate to the distinction between self-motion and the motion of others (based on the work of Bregman and others in auditory scene analysis), but this is little more than speculation. It would also be interesting to know what relationship there is between listeners' sense of virtual motion (and self-motion), and the *actual* motion (dancing, swaying, nodding, foot-tapping, etc.) that commonly accompanies listening and performing. Shove and Repp (1995) propose that a significant component of the sense of motion in music is derived from perceiving actual performance movements, but there has been no attempt yet to investigate the claim empirically. Equally, as the actions of "air guitar" players[5] may demonstrate, the actual movements that *listeners* make may play a part in eliciting, shaping, or intensifying virtual motion perception.

There are many more aspects of music perception which could be fruitfully studied using the basic approach of "what are the invariants that specify...?," but I will confine myself to three that relate to topics discussed elsewhere in this book, and one that goes in a slightly different direction. The first would be to investigate the invariants for various kinds of style categories, or musical structures. Asking the question, "what are the invariants that specify closure?," for example, could take advantage of previous research that has looked at harmonic tension and relaxation (e.g. Bigand and Parncutt 1999; Bigand, Parncutt, and Lerdahl 1996), but might open up a much more diverse enquiry that would encompass texture, rhythm, and melodic process as well. Since closure can be achieved in music that does not depend on tonal structure, a more stylistically wide-ranging approach might identify attributes that specify this common function beyond the narrow focus of tonal harmony. In a similar manner, Clarke and Dibben (1997) present a study that attempts to identify invariants for listeners' judgments of a number of functional categories in non-tonal music. Second, the discussion of subject position in chapter 4 suggests the possibility of an empirical investigation of the conditions that specify more or less engaged or alienated subject positions. I suggested in chapter 4 that in instrumental music (such as the Zappa guitar solo discussed there) the sense of a "distanced" subject position might be due to an awareness of surplus, excess, or disjunction of one sort or another between the musical subject matter and its treatment, and this is a suggestion that could be tackled empirically using music that falls somewhere along a continuum from the genuine to the parodic. Third, the claim is made in several places in this book that different kinds of sources (from instrument to ideology), do not differ in perceptual remoteness but perhaps in the temporal extent over which they are specified. It would be interesting to discover more about the duration of sound that is required for a person to identify different musical styles and, of course, the impact of various amounts and kinds of expertise on that attunement. Finally, the "what are the invariants that specify . . ." formula might be an interesting way to tackle the expressive properties of performance, building on and reinterpreting a great deal of previous work that has been carried out within various different conceptual frameworks. Juslin, Friberg and Bresin (2001–02), for instance, propose a number of interacting factors (Generative, Emotional, Random, Motional) as the primary components in performance expression. This and a body of other research on the production and perception of expression in performance, including the suggestions by Shove and Repp (1995) about performance movement and the sense of motion, could contribute to a wider investigation of what it is that the sounds of performance specify (for a preliminary discussion see Clarke 2002).

Ecology and Analysis, Ecology and Hermeneutics

Having considered some of the ways in which an ecological approach might engage with mainstream psychology of music, is there a way in which the ecological approach might relate to music analysis and hermeneutics? The discussions of the musical examples in this book are one demonstration of a way in which ecologically influenced music analysis might be approached. An implication of the ecological approach, as I've already argued, is to pay careful attention to musical materials—and from a perspective that is slightly different from the score-based orthodoxy of the past. For nonliterate traditions (such as most kinds of pop music) an ecological perspective suggests different ways to approach sound, as discussed above. But this looks rather like ecological theory driving analysis, and as Agawu (2000) argues, there is a potential circularity in that approach. Agawu's target is analysis driven by music theory (rather than ecological theory), but the point is the same: analysis, he aruges, should remain an essentially speculative activity that, in resisting the constraints of theory, retains a critical capacity.

> When foundations are enshrined in Theory and deployed in something called Theory-based analysis, they do nothing but reproduce themselves. It would be wise, then, in seeking to escape the circularity of theory-based analysis . . . to consider detaching theory from analysis. Theory is closed, analysis open. A theory-based analysis does not push at frontiers in the way that a non-theory-based one does. Theory is foundational, analysis non-foundational. But analysis is also performance, and its claims are to a different order of knowledge than, say, historical or archival knowledge. Analytical knowledge is non-cumulative whereas theoretical knowledge is cumulative. So it is possible that we would be doing analysis a favor by detaching it from theory in order to pursue both with equal commitment. (Agawu 2000: [26])

Agawu's appeal for analysis to be allowed to be "speculative" and not hidebound, and for "grand theories" of one sort or another to keep their potentially totalizing grasp to themselves, amounts to a claim for the hermeneutic and performative nature of analysis—and in this respect Agawu's position is shared by many other analysts and musicologists, among them Cook, Kramer, and McClary, for example. But elsewhere in the same commentary, he raises a rather more controversial question—specifically in relation to semiotics, in this case, but applying equally to other theoretical realignments, including the ecological approach that this book has developed. "Fundamental questions remain as to what semiotics [or ecological theory] finally achieves," states Agawu: "Is it a way of framing what we know already, or can it release first-order musical insights?" (Agawu 2000: [7]) The question is a good one—though the distinction between "first-order" musical insights and other (by implication "lower-order") insights is provocative. It is true that in the relationship between analysis and a newly applied theory[6] there can be a danger of being temporarily impressed by a substitution of terminology, or a reframing of some other kind, only to discover that nothing really has changed. But it is also worth considering what that framing, or reframing, might be able to achieve. First, it might generate specific empirical predictions (like those discussed above) that can then be explored—an outcome that *analysts*, admittedly, may not get too excited about, but which is nonetheless an opportunity for new insights into music more generally. Second, it may reveal relationships that were previously hidden and even unsuspected—such as the relationships between different invariants for closure—simply by virtue of framing previous discoveries in different terms. Third, it may genuinely help to explain phenomena that were previously inexplicable, by presenting them in terms of quite different elements and within a different conceptual framework. In short, I am not convinced that there really is a distinction between first-order and lesser-order musical insights. I think it may come down to what people think is *interesting*—which is quite a different matter, and a function of people's broader aims and agendas.

Similarly, I would argue that perceptual theory can make a contribution to a basically hermeneutic approach to music. As the theory and practice of interpretation, hermeneutics might appear to be incompatible with ecology, but the ecological approach can provide a "grounding" which, limiting hermeneutics' room for maneuver, helps to avoid the vicious circle that potentially undermines it. If everything is interpretation, then there are no constraints and we're all in a relativistic free-for-all in which the loudest or ideologically most powerful voice dominates. What Cook (2002) calls the "Scylla and Charybdis" of inherent versus socially constructed theories of meaning in music can be avoided by recognizing that ecological principles can help to explain why interpretations don't just spread unchecked in every possible direction. Cook's own approach to this problem uses the idea of basically iconic relationships (he calls them "enabling similarities") between properties of the musical material and the socially constructed meanings with which they come into correspondence, but applied with a flexibility and reciprocal influence that avoids some of the problems of the homological theories that he criticizes. Zbikowski (2002) uses metaphor theory, cross-domain mapping, and conceptual blending to achieve a somewhat similar outcome. Ecological theory offers the possibility of a different approach, based on the principle of affordance, and it is to this important concept—already discussed in chapter 1—that the next section returns.

The Affordances of Music and the Enactment of Musical Meaning

Gibson coined the term "affordance" to stand for the opportunities, functions, and values that a perceiver detects in the environment, arising from the mutual relationship between the needs and capacities of the organism, and the properties of objects and events. In the specific context of musical hermeneutics, musical material can be conceived as affording certain kinds of interpretations and not others. The much discussed recapitulation in the first movement of Beethoven's Ninth Symphony that Cook (2002) uses as an example for his own approach, affords interpretation both as "murderous sexual rage" (McClary 1991) and "the heavens on fire" (Tovey 1935–39, cited in Cook 2002), but not, for instance, as "world-weary indifference"; and the reason that it affords the first two interpretations but not the third is both because the music has particular material properties and because the interpretations have certain semantic requirements. Indifference and world-weariness have semantic requirements which this material cannot meet.

The term "affordance" has been used by other authors in relation to musical meaning (e.g. Cook 1998a; DeNora 2000), but not in ways that really preserve the radical, but problematic, sense that Gibson intended (Windsor 2000; 2002). Central to the concept is the idea that the perceiver/event relationship affords action—a reflection of the more general ecological principle of the reciprocity of perception and action (see chapter 1). In this sense, my own use of the term in the paragraph above appears decidedly nonstandard, even aberrant, referring as it does to the relationship between musical material and a socially constructed interpretation. But interpretation is also action—the speaking, writing, gesturing, and grimacing in which interpretation is manifest. To be more accurate, then (and a bit pedantic), the recapitulation of the first movement of Beethoven's Ninth Symphony affords writing (or speaking) about in terms of murderous sexual rage, or the heavens on fire.

Interpretative writing and speaking *are* forms of action, but of a comparatively discreet kind. In musicology they play a crucial role—indeed they more or less constitute the discipline—but in the wider world a whole range of other actions is afforded by music, and it is these that play the more central role in most people's lives. Music affords dancing, singing (and singing along), playing (and playing along), working, persuading, drinking and eating, doing aerobics, taking drugs, playing air guitar, traveling, protesting, seducing, waiting on the telephone, sleeping . . . the list is endless. These, as well as writing and speaking are what music affords, and what they demonstrate is the enacted character of musical meaning (see Iyer 2002). I have chosen to concentrate on the *perception* of musical meaning in this book (as its subtitle declares), because I am interested in explaining the experiences of so-called passive musical listening, a kind of listening that is typical of only a small proportion of listening even in Western culture. Even here it is an illusion: there really is no such thing as passive listening, or the "rapt contemplation" that is its more loftily expressed counterpart, but only different varieties of more or less concealed or sublimated active engagement. Nonetheless, the Western art music tradition, with its sharp division of musical labor (specialist composers, performers, and listeners), and the listening style with which it has become entwined, has had a cultural influence that vastly exceeds its actual currency. My concentration in this book on the perceptual side of the perception/action relationship is symptomatic of my own enculturation in that tradition and the influence it has had both on my own thinking and on the theories and practices of musicology and the psychology of music. In a wider perspective, however, this book should be no more than a part of a larger project on the *enactment* of musical meaning.

The myth of passive listening is strongest where music presents itself (or is socially constructed) as having no function: in other words within the ideology of autonomy. In various guises, the question of autonomy is the most persistently recurring theme of this book: the closed world of "purely musical sounds," and the source-specifying sounds of everyday listening; the "special" internal world of heightened subjectivity—idealized, escapist perhaps, a site of particular intensity; its virtual motion and virtual space; late Beethoven; the all-pervasive acousmatic presentation of music—each of these stands in relation to autonomy in one way or another. As a cultural construction, the idea of autonomy continues to perform a powerful ideological role, both as a barrier and a dynamic force in the critical power of music. While autonomy and ecology seem so incompatible, ecological theory provides a way to understand how music is able to move seamlessly between autonomy and heteronomy by means of the same perceptual mechanisms: sounds specify and afford—and can specify and afford sources and actions which are either predominantly immanent to the musical material or are predominantly "worldly."

In discussing autonomy I have tried to show how some aspects of people's listening experiences in relation to this music are amenable to an ecological analysis, but nonetheless the autonomy to which this music aspires—the self-sufficient integration that is both illusory and true—is at odds with the fundamentally practical and survival-driven character of an ecological perspective. Because ecology is first and foremost about adapting to, and conforming with, the world, it runs diametrically counter to the idea of art as critique. The critical value of art, from almost any perspective, is a function of its resistance to current conditions, its refusal to conform to easy adaptation. If the ecological ideal is the optimally efficient mutual adaptation of organism and environment, then it is against this background assumption that music achieves its uncomfortable and critical power. It constitutes a virtual environment in which "easy adaptation" is explored, manipulated, and deliberately thwarted in contrast to the ecological premise of adaptation towards conformity.

In the end, because music is the product of socialized and empirical human beings, there is no avoiding the "worldliness" of music, though that worldliness can be suspended, or seem to be suspended, with the willing collusion of listeners. Music affords ways of listening that extend from the mundane to the transcendent, from the inertia of being held on the telephone to the sound of a Haydn symphony, to the knife-edge responsiveness of co-performers—and ecological theory provides a way to understand and explore that diversity.

Notes ∿

INTRODUCTION

1. The writings of John Cage (1973), Murray Schafer (1977), Barry Truax (1984), and David Toop (1995) are some of the better-known exceptions.
2. Activity in the peripheral auditory system is necessary, but clearly not sufficient, for auditory perception.
3. For a critical review of Handel's book from an ecological perspective, see Heine and Guski (1991).
4. Some examples are Balzano (1986), Jones and Hahn (1986), Clarke (1987), Casey (1998), Nonken (1999), Dibben (2001), and Reybrouck (2001).

CHAPTER I

1. Taking a somewhat different approach from the one that I present here, Kaipainen (1996) also discusses the relationship between musical ecology and connectionism.
2. For two collections of writing on music and connectionism see Todd and Loy (1991) and Griffith and Todd (1999).
3. Successful connectionist models have been created that can be trained to make this kind of judgment, though the particular example that I discuss here is imaginary.

4. Clearly there is a "scale" of similarity to be considered here: identical events will lead to highly self-similar states of the system, though even this will depend on what else has happened in the interim, and what effect it has had on the organization of the system as a whole. And depending on how finely tuned the system is to particular environmental features, different degrees of similarity between one environmental event and another will result in more or less similar perceptual states.

5. This "disdain" is exploited in the joke that asks: what's the difference between a violin and a viola? To which the reply is: a viola takes longer to burn.

6. For a closely related and wide-ranging discussion, explicitly influenced by Gibson's writing, see Clark (1997).

7. In other musical cultures, such as South Indian classical music, there is not the sharp discontinuity between "tuning" and "playing" that is observed in Western classical music practice, where a period of silence and inactivity on the part of the performers invariably intervenes between the two.

CHAPTER 2

1. The timing of events in the recording (as with other recorded examples elsewhere in this book) is shown as minutes:seconds from the start of the track.

2. Leslie loudspeakers, often used by electric organ players and more occasionally by guitarists, have physically rotating loudspeaker cones, powered by electric motors, which causes the sound to appear to come and go as the cone first faces towards, and then rotates away from, a listener.

3. This is potentially a serious problem, since it opens a Pandora's box of individual listener differences and sensitivities. There might be two responses to this: one would be to take the problem seriously and literally, and either to offer an indefinite number of analyses based on a real or imagined assessment of the sensitivities of different listeners, or to undertake the ethnographic research that would document different listeners' *actual* perceptions, as DeNora (2000, chapter 2) has suggested; another would be to make an assumption about the shared or common sensitivities of a generalized audi-

ence to which the analysis is directed. This is essentially how most analysis is presented—though usually without being explicit about the assumption, and often with an idealized or unrealistically expert readership in mind.

4. This is neither for spuriously purist reasons, nor out of a belief in musical absolutism but for the more pragmatic reason that this is how I (and presumably many other people) came to know the track.

5. Beyond this single reference to the drum kit, the analysis that follows will be restricted to a discussion of the guitar sounds, since the bass and kit play a subordinate and essentially supporting role in the performance.

6. Once again the circumstances of listening are crucial: for a listener hearing the CD 35 years or more after the performance itself, these sounds have specifications that are somewhat different from those to which the live audience at Woodstock in 1969 would have been sensitive.

7. I am grateful to an anonymous reviewer for pointing this out to me.

8. In a further twist on this passage, a second anonymous reader pointed out that "the quote of 'Taps' is also quite natural for any guitarist, who would have learned to play the tune on pure harmonics (strings 4, 3, and 2 at the twelfth fret supply almost all the notes for the tune—the high note is available on the seventh fret of the third string)." This reader/listener hears the way in which the sounds specify the guitarist's physical engagement with the instrument, an example of the close relationship between perception and action.

CHAPTER 3

1. The words "motion" and "movement" have been used in a partially interchangeable manner within the literature on music. In an attempt to be consistent, and to respect potentially important distinctions, I will use "motion" to denote the abstract category of spatial displacement in time, and "movement" to denote specific examples of particular spatial displacements.

2. In terms of physics, of course, sound is always the vibratory movement of the molecules of the medium—but this is an ecologically irrelevant level of description.

3. This claim of course excludes the tangible sense of the real space within which music is performed (and the possible movements of instrumentalists in that space), picked up by a listener either visually or auditorily.

4. A rather direct equivalent to M. C. Escher's well-known lithograph from 1960 entitled "Ascending and Descending" (in which two lines of monkish figures endlessly ascend and descend the same paradoxical staircase) is the illusion of endless ascent or descent in pitch that can be created using so-called Shepard tones. By using sounds with only octave-spaced harmonics, a stepwise semitonal sequence seems always to rise (or fall) only to appear to be back in the same place (see Shepard 1964).

5. The effect, and the conditions required to create it, is analogous to the phenomenon known as melodic fusion or fission, discussed extensively in Bregman (1990).

6. Acousmatic music is music presented over loudspeakers or headphones without any real-world source being visible. While any music that is presented over loudspeakers or headphones conforms with this definition (including, for example, conventional instrumental music heard on a domestic hi-fi), Windsor's discussion has most force in its consideration of music that is made specifically for acousmatic presentation—electroacoustic music most obviously.

7. LaMonte Young's piece *Composition 1960 no. 7*, for example, which consists simply of a perfect fifth B/F# "to be held for a very long time," is an extreme example of the latter (stasis).

8. As Adlington (2003) has pointed out in a discussion of the metaphor of motion, change in music doesn't necessarily need to be heard as motion. But motion certainly cannot be heard in the absence of change.

9. Available on Polygram CD B00000E53D.

10. See Bregman (1990).

11. The six-note chord into which the first crescendo "collides" is the chord associated with Wozzeck's own death two scenes later.

12. The powerful motional and spatial character of some electroacoustic music, and other varieties of electronic music, provide examples of this.

CHAPTER 4

1. Lyrics listed at http://www.oldielyrics.com/lyrics/frank_zappa/magdalena.html
2. Caused literally by a tightening of the vocal tract.
3. Some of the tokens of this conventional façade are that elsewhere in the song we learn that the wife/mother is out at a bridge party, that the mother and daughter go shopping at department stores together, that the father watches the Johnny Carson show on television, and that the interior of the house is replete with a picture of Jesus and sparklets machine.
4. No attempt has been made to notate this in the example.
5. Although this is, of course, precisely where the illusion has been created.
6. The credits on the CD read: "Words written and sung by Polly Jean Harvey. Music written and played by John Parish."
7. The word is problematic: what I intend by it here is that the style does not make use of self-conscious stylistic borrowing as a primary device.
8. A pattern that is reproduced in the tonal trajectory of the movement as whole.

CHAPTER 5

1. See e.g. Keller (1985).
2. Salzer's (1962) book is actually entitled *Structural Hearing*.
3. It is ironic that, as Chua (1999) points out, the term "absolute music" was first used by Wagner, perhaps the greatest champion in the nineteenth century of nonabsolute music, in a review of Beethoven's Ninth Symphony, a work that breaks with symphonic absolutism.
4. The apparently "impatient" behavior of children, not yet socialized into the peculiar kinds of disengagement, inactivity, or silence that these contexts require, is just one indicator of how strange the situation is. And this "impatience" cannot simply be reduced to some crude idea of their developmentally limited attention span; these same children will happily spend hours playing with one another or on their own with a toy or game with

which they can continuously interact—even fiddling about with a musical instrument!

5. See Windsor (2000) and Dibben (2001; 2003) for further discussion.

6. Perhaps the way in which viewers at an art gallery tilt their head on one side when looking at a painting is some kind of residual attempt to get a different perspective (literal, spatial, perspective) on the scene/object in front of them in the expectation that this will help them to see what it is, or what it means.

7. This kind of dancing is usually unchoreographed in the sense that it has not been extensively worked out in advance (and certainly not by someone other than the dancer, as would be the case in classical ballet or modern dance). But it may be stylized to varying degrees and will certainly incorporate elements of the common culture of dancing—the dance equivalent of musical topics.

8. Though as has been widely observed, people have an extraordinary capacity to extend the site of their perceptual experience beyond the confines of their body. When a person pokes a stick into the hot ashes of a fire, she feels the texture of the ashes and cinders *at the end of the stick*—not where her fingers grip it. In the same way, a pianist feels the hammer hit the string (despite the complex chain of physical linkages between the key and the hammer) instead of (or perhaps as well as) the finger touching the key.

9. I am not referring here to the way that the hand/finger may be guided to the right place by a deliberate process of auditory feedback (i.e. sliding relatively slowly up the string until the player can hear that she has "got there"), but rather to the almost miraculous way that a rapid (i.e. apparently ballistic) shift seems to hit the target infinitely more reliably when you can *hear* what you are aiming at.

CHAPTER 6

1. I vividly remember hearing a new work for solo piano at a concert, at the end of which my neighbor remarked to me how much he had enjoyed the "fairground music" in the piece. Listening in a rather unfocused manner, I hadn't been aware of hearing anything more than "contemporary piano music."

2. The subsequent denials by members of the band that the song had anything to do with LSD make no difference to the fact that most listeners at the time thought that *they* knew what it was about.

3. Though the minor key is, of course, characteristic of funeral marches.

4. Tagg and Clarida (2003) provide a detailed account of precisely this kind of evidence for a very different musical repertory.

5. Hatten (2001) presents a similar list of possible modern and post-modern interpretations of the movement.

6. There are other such relationships (the cello's reordered statement of its own material in bars 5–6, and its marginally rhythmically altered repetition of the first violin material from 3–4 in bars 7–8, and a number of others) that give the material as a whole a sense of homogeneity.

7. The cello and viola actually double at the octave for some of this, but the effect is one of timbre more than pitch.

8. The flat supertonic, functioning as Neapolitan harmony, is itself an intensification of this basic tonic-dominant orientation.

9. There is an interesting question here about what it is that specifies the tempo of music (see e.g. Drake, Gros, and Penel 1999). One factor is simply the rate of change of the fastest moving musical dimension (pitch change, or some other means of articulation), and another (in tonal music particularly) is the rate of harmonic change.

10. Virgin Classics: CD7243 5 61406 2 2.

11. The "dual" language that I use from here to the end of the paragraph is an attempt to convey this subject/object indeterminacy.

12. By limiting my analysis of structural process to just the first 21 bars a great deal more in the way of "formal uncertainty" is missed, but the basic point is made.

13. Among them Kerman (1979), Chua (1995), Spitzer (1999), McClary (2000), and Hatten (2001).

CONCLUSION

1. Note that this exposes two complementary ways to understand perception and meaning that have so far been rather more tacit than explicit. For much of the book I have discussed what it is that sounds *specify* for listeners, which emphasizes the direction *from*

sound to objects, events, and practices, and focuses on the invariants that are responsible for such specification (the study of perception). The complementary, and equivalent, formulation is to consider the *sources* of sounds (again objects, events, and practices), which draws attention to the origins of sounds and focuses on the ways in which objects, events, and practices are manifest in sound (the study of sonic culture).

2. Indeed at the start of the first movement of Beethoven's Op. 132 string quartet this is likely to be the case, given the gradual manner in which the members of the quartet join the texture. Identification of a particular string quartet is also, of course, a function of perceptual expertise: many more listeners have had repeated experience of the specific sound of the cello and its distinguishing characteristics than have had enough exposure to the Borodin String Quartet to distinguish it from other string quartets.

3. Examples might be Lerdahl and Jackendoff (1983), Krumhansl (1990), Dowling and Harwood (1986), and Temperley (2001).

4. A paper by Gabrielsson (1973) is an important precursor in this respect but, as noted in chapter 3, it makes use of only highly simplified pitchless rhythms.

5. And not only air guitar players, of course: even in quite formal circumstances, and across many different genres, listeners move in all kinds of ways that would repay detailed investigation.

6. Previous examples of this have included information theory in the 1960s and semiotics in the 1970s and 1980s.

References ~

Adlington, R. (2003) Moving beyond motion: metaphors for changing sound. *Journal of the Royal Musical Association*, 128, 297–318.

Adorno, T. W. (1976) *Introduction to the Sociology of Music* (Trans. E. B. Ashton). New York: The Seabury Press.

Agawu, K. (1991) *Playing with Signs. A Semiotic Interpretation of Classic Music*. Princeton, NJ: Princeton University Press.

———. (2000) Response to plenary session. *Music Theory Online*, 6 (1).

Allanbrook, W. J. (1983) *Rhythmic Gesture in Mozart. Le Nozze di Figaro & Don Giovanni*. Chicago: University of Chicago Press.

Baily, J. (1996) Using tests of sound perception in fieldwork. *Yearbook for Traditional Music*, 28, 147–173.

Balzano, G. (1982) The pitch set as a level of description for studying musical pitch perception. In M. Clynes, ed., *Music, Mind, and Brain. The Neuropsychology of Music*. New York and London: Plenum, 321–351.

———. (1986) Music perception as detection of pitch–time constraints. In V. McCabe and G. Balzano, eds., *Event Cognition: An Ecological Perspective*. Hillsdale, NJ: Lawrence Erlbaum, 217–233.

———. (1987) Measuring music. In A. Gabrielsson, ed., *Action and Perception in Rhythm and Music*. Stockholm: Publications of the Swedish Academy of Music, no. 55, 177–199.

Barker, A. (1989) *Greek Musical Writings, Volume II, Harmonic and Acoustic Theory*. Cambridge: Cambridge University Press.

Barthes, R. (1968) *Elements of Semiology* (Trans. A. Lavers and C. Smith). New York: Hill and Wang.

Benjamin, W. (1970) The Work of Art in the Age of Mechanical Reproduction. In *Illuminations* (Trans. H. Zohn). London: Fontana, 219–253.

Berliner, P. (1997) Give and take: The collective conversation of jazz performance. In R. K. Sawyer, ed., *Creativity in Performance*. Greenwich, CT: Ablex, 9–41.

Berry, W. (1976) *Structural Functions in Music*. Englewood Cliffs, NJ: Prentice Hall.

Bharucha, J. J. (1987) Music cognition and perceptual facilitation: a connectionist framework. *Music Perception*, 5, 1–30.

———. (1991a) Pitch, harmony, and neural nets: a psychological perspective. In P. M. Todd and D. G. Loy (Eds) (1991) *Music and Connectionism*. Cambridge, MA: MIT Press, 84–99.

———. (1991b) Cognitive and brain mechanisms in perceptual learning. In J. Sundberg, L. Nord, and R. Carlson, eds., *Music, Language, Speech and Brain*. Basingstoke: Macmillan, 349–358.

———. (1999) Neural nets, temporal composites, and tonality. In D. Deutsch, ed., *The Psychology of Music*, 2d Ed. San Diego: Academic Press, 413–440.

Bharucha, J. J., and Stoeckig, K. (1987) Priming of chords: spreading activation or overlapping frequency spectra? *Perception & Psychophysics*, 41, 519–524.

Bharucha, J. J., and Todd, P. M. (1991) Modeling the perception of tonal structure with neural nets. In P. M. Todd and D. G. Loy, eds., *Music and Connectionism*. Cambridge, MA: MIT Press, 128–137.

Bigand, E., and Parncutt, R. (1999) Perception of musical tension in long chord sequences. *Psychological Research*, 62, 237–254.

Bigand, E., Parncutt, R., and Lerdahl, F. (1996) Perception of musical tension in short chord sequences: the influence of harmonic function, sensory dissonance, horizontal motion, and musical training. *Perception & Psychophysics*, 58, 125–141.

Boros, J. (1995) A "New Totality"? *Perspectives of New Music*, 31, 538–553.

Bohlmann, P. V. (1999) Ontologies of music. In N. Cook and M. Everist, eds., *Rethinking Music*. Oxford: Oxford University Press, 17–34.

Bregman, A. S. (1990) *Auditory Scene Analysis. The Perceptual Organiza-tion of Sound.* Cambridge, MA: MIT Press.

Butler, D. (1989) Describing the perception of tonality in music: a cri-tique of the tonal hierarchy theory and a proposal for a theory of intervallic rivalry. *Music Perception,* 6, 219–241.

Cage, J. (1973) *Silence. Lectures and Writings.* London: Calder and Boyars.

Casey, M. (1998) Auditory Group Theory with Applications to Statistical Basis Methods for Structured Audio. Unpublished PhD thesis, Mas-sachusetts Institute of Technology.

Chua, D. (1995) *The "Galitzin" Quartets of Beethoven : Opp. 127, 132, 130.* Princeton, NJ: Princeton University Press

Chua, D. K. L. (1999) *Absolute Music and the Construction of Meaning.* Cambridge: Cambridge University Press.

Clark, A. (1997) *Being There. Putting Brain, Body, and World Together Again.* Cambridge, MA: MIT Press.

Clarke, D. I. (2003) Musical autonomy revisited. In M. Clayton, T. Her-bert, and R. Middleton, eds., *The Cultural Study of Music: A Critical Introduction.* London: Routledge, 159–170.

Clarke, E. F. (1987) Categorical rhythm perception: an ecological per-spective. In A. Gabrielsson, ed., *Action and Perception in Rhythm and Music.* Stockholm: Publications of the Swedish Academy of Music, no. 55, 19–33.

———. (1999) Rhythm and timing in music. In D. Deutsch (Ed.) *The Psychology of Music,* 2d Ed. New York: Academic Press, 473–500.

———. (2002) Listening to performance. In J. Rink, ed., *Musical Perfor-mance. A Guide to Understanding.* Cambridge: Cambridge Univer-sity Press, 185–196.

———. (2003) Music and Psychology. In M. Clayton, T. Herbert, and R. Middleton, eds., *The Cultural Study of Music. A Critical Introduc-tion.* London: Routledge, 113–123.

Clarke, E. F., and Davidson, J. W. (1998) The Body in Performance. In W. Thomas, ed., *Composition—Performance—Reception. Studies in the Creative Process in Music.* Aldershot: Ashgate Press, 74–92.

Clarke, E. F., and Dibben, N. (1997) An ecological approach to simi-larity and categorisation in music. In M. Ramscar, U. Hahn, E. Cambouropolos, and H. Pain, eds., *Proceedings of SimCat 1997:*

An Interdisciplinary Workshop on Similarity and Categorisation.
Edinburgh: Department of Artificial Intelligence, Edinburgh University, 37–41.

Clayton, M. (2001) Introduction: towards a theory of musical meaning (in India and elsewhere). *British Journal of Ethnomusicology*, 10, 1–17.

Clifton, T. (1983) *Music as Heard. A Study in Applied Phenomenology.* New Haven and London: Yale University Press.

Clynes, M. (1977) *Sentics: The Touch of Emotions.* New York: Doubleday.

———. (1983) Expressive microstructure in music, linked to living qualities. In J. Sundberg, ed., *Studies of Music Performance.* Stockholm: Publications of The Royal Swedish Academy of Music, no. 39, 76–181.

Cogan, R. (1984) *New Images of Musical Sound.* Cambridge, MA: Harvard University Press.

Cooke, D. (1959) *The Language of Music.* Oxford: Oxford University Press.

Cook, N. (1990) *Music, Imagination and Culture.* Oxford: Oxford University Press.

———. (1994) Perception: A Perspective from Music Theory. In R. Aiello and J. A. Sloboda, eds., *Musical Perceptions.* New York: Oxford University Press, 64–95.

———. (1998a) *Analysing Musical Multimedia.* Oxford: The Clarendon Press.

———. (1998b) *Music. A Very Short Introduction.* Oxford: Oxford University Press.

———. (2002) Theorizing musical meaning. *Music Theory Spectrum,* 23, 170–195.

Cook, N., and Dibben, N. (2001) Musicological approaches to music and emotion. In P. N. Juslin and J. A. Sloboda, eds., *Music and Emotion. Theory and Research.* Oxford: Oxford University Press, 45–70.

Costall, A. (1991) 'Graceful degradation': Cognitivism and the metaphors of the computer. In A. Still and A. Costall, eds., *Against Cognitivism. Alternative Foundations for Cognitive Psychology.* London: Harvester Wheatsheaf, 151–169.

Croft, J. (1999) Musical Memory, Complexity, and Lerdahl's Cognitive Constraints. Unpublished MMus. Dissertation, University of Sheffield.

Cross, I. (2003) Music and Biocultural Evolution. In M. Clayton, T. Herbert, and R. Middleton, eds., *The Cultural Study of Music: A Critical Introduction*. London: Routledge, 19–30.

Crowder, R. G. (1993) Auditory memory. In S. McAdams and E. Bigand, eds., *Thinking in Sound. The Cognitive Psychology of Human Audition*. Oxford: Clarendon Press, 113–145.

Csikszentmihalyi, M. (1990) *Flow: The Psychology of Optimal Experience.* New York: Harper and Row.

Cumming, N. (2000) *The Sonic Self. Musical Subjectivity and Signification*. Bloomington and Indianapolis: Indiana University Press.

Dahlhaus, C. (1987) On the decline of the concept of the musical work. In *Schoenberg and the New Music. Essays by Carl Dahlhaus* (Trans. D. Puffett and A. Clayton). Cambridge: Cambridge University Press, 234–247.

————. (1989) *Nineteenth Century Music* (Trans. J. Bradford Robinson). Berkeley: University of California Press.

Davies, S. (1994) *Musical Meaning and Expression*. Ithaca, NY: Cornell University Press.

Dempster, D. (1994) How Does Debussy's Sea Crash? How Can Jimi's Rocket Red Glare?: Kivy's Account of Representation in Music. *The Journal of Aesthetics and Art Criticism*, 52, 415–428.

DeNora, T. (2000) *Music in Everyday Life*. Cambridge: Cambridge University Press.

Deutsch, D. (1999): The processing of pitch combinations. In D. Deutsch, ed., *The Psychology of Music*, 2d Ed. New York: Academic Press, 349–411.

Dibben, N. (1996) The Role of Reductional Representations in the Perception of Atonal Music. Unpublished PhD thesis, University of Sheffield.

————. (2001) What do we hear when we hear music? Music perception and musical material. *Musicae Scientiae*, 5, 161–194.

————. (2003) Musical Materials, Perception, and Listening. In M. Clayton, T. Herbert, and R. Middleton, eds., *The Cultural Study of Music: A Critical Introduction*. London: Routledge, 193–203.

Dowling, W. J., and Harwood, D. L. (1986) *Music Cognition*. New York: Academic Press.

———. (1989) Simplicity and complexity in music and cognition. *Contemporary Music Review*, 4, 247–253.

Drabkin, W. (1985) Beethoven and the open string. *Music Analysis*, 4, 15–29.

Drake, C., Gros, L., and Penel, A. (1999) How fast is that music? The relation between physical and perceived tempo. In Suk Won Yi, ed., *Music, Mind and Science*. Seoul: Seoul National University Press, 190–203.

Eco, U. (1977) *A Theory of Semiotics*. London and Basingstoke: Macmillan.

Eno, B. (1996) *A Year with Swollen Appendices*. London: Faber and Faber.

Everett, W. (1999) *The Beatles as Musicians* New York: Oxford University Press.

Fatboy Slim (1998) "Build It Up, Tear It Down." *You've Come a Long Way, Baby*. Skint Records: Skint 11.

Feld, S. (1994) From Ethnomusicology to Echo–Muse–Ecology: Reading R. Murray Schafer in the Papua New Guinea Rainforest. The Soundscape Newsletter, 8. Reproduced at http://interact.uoregon.edu/Medialit/wfae/readings/ecomuse.html.

Flach, J. M., and Smith, M. R. H. (2000) Right Strategy, Wrong Tactic. *Ecological Psychology*, 12, 43–51.

Gabrielsson, A. (1973) Adjective ratings and dimension analyses of auditory rhythm patterns. *Scandinavian Journal of Psychology*, 14, 244–260.

Gaver, W. W. (1993a) What in the world do we hear?: an ecological approach to auditory event perception. *Ecological Psychology*, 5, 1–29.

———. (1993b) How do we hear in the world?: explorations in ecological acoustics. *Ecological Psychology*, 5, 285–313.

Gibson, E. J. (1969) *Principles of Perceptual Learning and Development*. New York: Appleton–Century–Crofts.

Gibson, J. J. (1958) Visually controlled locomotion and visual orientation in animals. *British Journal of Psychology*, 49, 182–194.

———. (1966) *The Senses Considered as Perceptual Systems*. Boston: Houghton Mifflin.

———. (1979) *The Ecological Approach to Visual Perception*. Hillsdale, NJ: Lawrence Erlbaum.

Gibson, J. J., and Gibson, E. J. (1955) Perceptual learning: differentiation or enrichment? *Psychological Review*, 62, 32–41.

Gjerdingen, R. O. (1999) Apparent motion in music? In N. Griffith and P. Todd, eds., *Musical Networks. Parallel Distributed Perception and Performance*. Cambridge, MA: MIT Press, 141–173.

Goehr, L. (1992) *The Imaginary Museum of Musical Works: An Essay in the Philosophy of Music*. Oxford: The Clarendon Press.

Green, L. (1988) *Music on Deaf Ears: Musical Meaning, Ideology and Education*. Manchester: Manchester University Press.

———. (2005) Musical experience and social reproduction: a case for retrieving autonomy. *Educational Philosophy and Theory*, 37, 75–90.

Gregory, R. L. (1987) Plasticity in the nervous system. In R. L. Gregory, ed., *The Oxford Companion to the Mind*. Oxford: Oxford University Press, 623–628.

Griffith, N., and Todd, P., eds. (1999) *Musical Networks. Parallel Distributed Perception and Performance*. Cambridge, MA: MIT Press.

Grossberg, S. (1982) *Studies of Mind and Brain: Neural Principles of Learning, Perception, Development, Cognition, and Motor Control*. Boston: Reidel/Kluwer.

Handel, S. (1989) *Listening: An Introduction to the Perception of Auditory Events*. Cambridge, MA: MIT Press.

Hargreaves, D. J., and Coleman, A. M. (1981) The dimensions of aesthetic reactions to music. *Psychology of Music*, 9, 15–19.

Hatten, R. S. (2001) Interpreting the first movement of Beethoven's Op. 132: The limits of modernist and postmodernist analogies. Paper presented at the conference "Beethoven and the Music of the 20th Century, Century of Apocalypse and Hope," Music Academy of Krakow, Poland; April 11–12, 2001.

———. (1994) *Musical Meaning in Beethoven. Markedness, Correlation, and Interpretation*. Bloomington and Indianapolis: Indiana University Press.

Hedden, S. K. (1973) Listeners' responses to music in relation to autochthonous and experiential factors. *Journal of Research in Music Education*, 21, 225–238.

Heft, H. (2001) *Ecological Psychology in Context: James Gibson, Roger Barker, and the Legacy of William James's Radical Empiricism*. Mahwah, NJ: Lawrence Erlbaum.

Heine, W.-D., and Guski, R. (1991) Listening: The perception of auditory events? An essay review of *Listening: An Introduction to the Perception of Auditory Events* by Stephen Handel. *Ecological Psychology*, 3, 263–275.

Hurley, S., and Noë, A. (2003) Neural plasticity and consciousness. *Biology and Philosophy*, 18, 131–168.

Iyer, V. (2002) Embodied mind, situated cognition, and expressive microtiming in African-American music. *Music Perception*, 19, 387–414.

James, W. (1892) *Psychology: Briefer Course*. New York: Henry Holt and Co.

Johnson, J. H. (1995) *Listening in Paris: a Cultural History*. Berkeley: University of California Press.

Johnson, J. J. (2002) *Who Needs Classical Music? Cultural Choice and Musical Value*. New York: Oxford University Press.

Johnston, S. (1985) Film narrative and the structuralist controversy. In P. Cook, ed., *The Cinema Book*. London: British Film Institute, 221–250.

Jones, M. R., and Hahn, J. (1986) Invariants in sound. In V. McCabe and G. Balzano, eds., *Event Cognition: An Ecological Perspective*. Hillsdale, NJ: Lawrence Erlbaum, 197–215.

Juslin, P. N., Friberg, A., and Bresin, R. (2001–2) Toward a computational model of expression in music performance: the GERM model. Special issue of *Musicae Scientiae: Current Trends in the Study of Music and Emotion*, 63–122.

Kahneman, D. (1973) *Attention and Effort*. Englewood Cliffs, NJ: Prentice–Hall.

Kaipainen, M. (1996) Representing and remotivating musical processes: modeling a recurrent musical ecology. *Journal of New Music Research*, 25, 150–178.

Keller, H. (1985) Functional analysis of Mozart's G Minor Quintet. *Music Analysis*, 4, 73–94.

Kemp, A. E. (1996) *The Musical Temperament*. Oxford: Oxford University Press.

Kerman, J. (1985) *Musicology*. London: Fontana.

Kerman, J. (1979) *The Beethoven String Quartets*. New York: W. W. Norton.

Kivy, P. (1990) *Music Alone: Philosophical Reflections on the Purely Musical Experience*. Ithaca, NY: Cornell University Press.

Kohonen, T. (1984) *Self-organization and Associative Memory*. Berlin: Springer Verlag.

Kolers, P. A. (1972) *Aspects of Motion Perception*. Oxford: Pergamon Press.

Kramer, L. (1995) *Classical Music and Postmodern Knowledge*. Berkeley: University of California Press.

———. (2002) *Musical Meaning: Toward a Critical History.* Berkeley: University of California Press.

———. (2003) Subjectivity Rampant! Music, Hermeneutics, and History. In M. Clayton, T. Herbert, and R. Middleton, eds., *The Cultural Study of Music. A Critical Introduction*. London: Routledge, 124–135.

Krumhansl, C. L. (1990) *Cognitive Foundations of Musical Pitch*. New York: Oxford University Press.

———. (1995) Music psychology and music theory: Problems and prospects. *Music Theory Spectrum*, 17, 53–90.

———. (1998) Topic in music: an empirical study of memorability, openness, and emotion in Mozart's string quintet in C major and Beethoven's string quartet in A minor. *Music Perception*, 16, 119–134.

Lakoff, G., and Johnson, M. (1980) *Metaphors We Live By*. Chicago: University of Chicago Press.

———. (1999) *Philosophy in the Flesh. The Embodied Mind and Its Challenge to Western Thought*. New York: Basic Books.

Langer, S. K. (1942) *Philosophy in a New Key*. Cambridge, MA: Harvard University Press.

Large, E. W., and Palmer, C. (2002) Temporal responses to music performance: Perceiving structure in temporal fluctuation. *Cognitive Science*, 26, 1–37

Lecanuet, J.-P. (1996) Prenatal auditory experience. In I. Deliège and J. Sloboda, eds., *Musical Beginnings. Origins and Development of Music*. Oxford: Oxford University Press, 3–34.

Lee, D. N. (1980) The optic flow field: the foundation of vision. *Philosophical Transactions of the Royal Society*, B290, 169–179.

Leman, M. (1991) The ontogenesis of tonal semantics: results of a computer study. In P. M. Todd and D. G. Loy, eds., *Music and Connectionism*. Cambridge, MA: MIT Press, 100–127.

Lerdahl, F. (1988) Cognitive constraints on compositional systems. In J. A. Sloboda, ed., *Generative Processes in Music. The Psychology of Performance, Improvisation, and Composition*. Oxford: The Clarendon Press, 231–259.

———. (1989) Atonal prolongational structure. *Contemporary Music Review*, 4, 65–87.

———. (2001) *Tonal Pitch Space*. New York: Oxford University Press.

Lerdahl, F., and Jackendoff, R. (1983) *A Generative Theory of Tonal Music*. Cambridge, MA: MIT Press.

Levy, J. (1982) Texture as a sign in classic and early romantic music. *Journal of the American Musicological Society*, 35, 482–531.

Lidov, D. (1987) Mind and body in music. *Semiotica*, 66, 69–97.

Martin, P. J. (1995) *Sounds and Society. Themes in the Sociology of Music*. Manchester: Manchester University Press.

McAdams, S. (1984) Spectral Fusion, Spectral Parsing, and the Formation of Auditory Images. Unpublished PhD thesis, Stanford University.

McClary, S. (1991) *Feminine Endings*. Minneapolis: University of Minnesota Press.

———. (2000) *Conventional Wisdom. The Content of Musical Form*. Berkeley: University of California Press.

Meidner, O. (1985) Motion and e–motion in music. *British Journal of Aesthetics*, 25, 349–356.

Meyer, L. B. (1956) *Emotion and Meaning in Music*. Chicago: University of Chicago Press.

Monelle, R. (1992) *Linguistics and Semiotics in Music*. Chur, Switzerland: Harwood Academic Publishers.

———. (2000) *The Sense of Music: Semiotic Essays*. Princeton, NJ: Princeton University Press.

Moore, B. C. J. (1997) *An Introduction to the Psychology of Hearing*. 4th Ed. London: Academic Press.

Nagel, T. (1982) What is it like to be a bat? In D. R. Hofstadter and D. C. Dennett, eds., *The Mind's I. Fantasies and Reflections on Self and Soul*. Harmondsworth: Penguin Books, 391–403.

Nattiez, J.-J. (1990) *Music and Discourse. Toward a Semiology of Music* (Trans. C. Abbate). Princeton, NJ: Princeton University Press.

Neisser, U. (1976) *Cognition and Reality*. San Francisco: W. H. Freeman and Co.

Noble, W. (1991) Ecological realism and the fallacy of 'objectification.' In A. Still and A. Costall, eds., *Against Cognitivism. Alternative Foundations for Cognitive Psychology*. London: Harvester Wheatsheaf, 199–224.

Noë, A. (2002) Art as Enaction. Art and Cognition Virtual Conference, accessed at http://www.interdisciplines.org/artcog/.

Nonken, M. C. (1999) An Ecological Approach to Music Perception: Stimulus–Driven Listening and the Complexity Repertoire. Unpublished PhD thesis, University of Columbia, New York.

Parncutt, R. (1989) *Harmony: A Psychoacoustical Approach*. Berlin and London: Springer–Verlag.

Piaget, J. (1977) *The Grasp of Consciousness. Action and Concept in the Young Child* (Trans. S. Wedgwood). London: Routledge.

Purkis, C. (1995) Postmodernity at the piano: 19th century erotic bodies and the limits of language. *Critical Musicology Newsletter*, 3, 34–40.

Ramachandran, V.S. (2000) Mirror neurons and imitation learning as the driving force behind "the great leap forward" in human evolution. Edge Website article http://www.edge.org/documents/archive/edge69.html.

Ratner, L. G. (1980) *Classic Music: Expression, Form, and Style.* New York: Schirmer Books.

Reed, E. S. (1988) *James J. Gibson and the Psychology of Perception.* New Haven and London: Yale University Press.

———. (1991) James Gibson's ecological approach to cognition. In A. Still and A. Costall (Eds.) *Against Cognitivism. Alternative Foundations for Cognitive Psychology*. London: Harvester Wheatsheaf, 171–198.

———. (1996) *Encountering the World. Toward an Ecological Psychology.* New York: Oxford University Press.

Reich, S. (1965) *It's Gonna Rain*. Recorded on Elektra/Nonesuch CD 979 169–2 (1987).

Repp, B. (1993) Music as motion: a synopsis of Alexander Truslit's (1938) "Gestaltung und Bewegung in der Musik." *Psychology of Music*, 21, 48–72.

Reybrouck, M. (2001) Biological roots of musical epistemology: Functional cycles, Umwelt, and enactive listening. *Semiotica*, 134, 599–633.

Rumelhart, D. E., and McClelland, J. L. (1986) *Parallel Distributed Processing: Explorations in the Microstructure of Cognition.* Cambridge, MA: MIT Press.

Salzer, F. (1962) *Structural Hearing. Tonal Coherence in Music.* New York: Dover.

Samson, J. (1999) Analysis in context. In N. Cook and M. Everist, eds., *Rethinking Music.* Oxford: Oxford University Press, 35–54.

Schafer, R. M. (1977) *The Tuning of the World.* New York: Knopf.

Scott, D., ed., (2000) *Music, Culture, and Society. A Reader.* Oxford: Oxford University Press.

Scruton, R. (1997) *The Aesthetics of Music.* Oxford: The Clarendon Press.

Serafine, M. L. (1988) *Music as Cognition. The Development of Thought in Sound.* New York: Columbia University Press.

Shepard, R. N. (1964) Circularity in judgments of relative pitch. *Journal of the Acoustical Society of America,* 36, 2346–2353.

Shove, P., and Repp, B. (1995) Musical motion and performance: theoretical and empirical perspectives. In J. Rink, ed., *The Practice of Performance. Studies in Musical Interpretation.* Cambridge: Cambridge University Press, 55–83.

Sloboda, J. A. (1991) Music structure and emotional response: some empirical findings. *Psychology of Music,* 19, 110–120.

Sloboda, J. A., O'Neill, S., and Ivaldi, A. (2001) Functions of music in everyday life: an exploratory study using the Experience Sampling Method. *Musicae Scientiae,* 5, 9–32.

Small, C. (1998) *Musicking: The Meanings of Performing and Listening.* Hanover: University Press of New England.

Smalley, D. (1986) Spectromorphology and structuring processes. In S. Emmerson, ed., *The Language of Electroacoustic Music.* Basingstoke: Macmillan, 61–93.

———. (1992) The listening imagination: listening in the electroacoustic era. In J. Paynter, T. Howell, R. Orton, and P. Seymour, eds., *Companion to Contemporary Musical Thought.* London: Routledge, 514–554.

———. (1997) Spectromorphology: explaining sound shapes. *Organised Sound,* 2, 107–126.

Smith, G. (1995) *Lost in Music.* London: Picador.

Smith, J. D. (1987) Conflicting aesthetic ideals in a musical culture. *Music Perception*, 4, 373–392.

Spice, N. (1995) Hubbub. *London Review of Books*, July 6 1995, 3–6.

Spitzer, M. (1999) Inside Beethoven's "Magic Square." The Structural Semantics of Op. 132. In C. Miereanu, ed., *Les Universaux en Musique*. Paris: Publications de la Sorbonne, 87–125.

Still, A., and Costall, A., eds., (1991) *Against Cognitivism. Alternative Foundations for Cognitive Psychology*. London: Harvester Wheatsheaf.

Subotnik, R. R. (1988) Toward a deconstruction of structural listening: a critique of Schoenberg, Adorno, and Stravinsky. In E. Narmour and R. Solie, eds., *Explorations in Music, the Arts, and Ideas: Essays in Honor of Leonard B. Meyer*. Stuyvesant, NY: Pendragon Press, 87–122.

Sudnow, D. (2001) *Ways of the Hand: A Rewritten Account*. Cambridge, MA: MIT Press.

Sutcliffe, W. D. (1987) Haydn's piano trio textures. *Music Analysis*, 6, 319–332.

———. (2003) Haydn, Mozart and their contemporaries. In R. Stowell, ed., *The Cambridge Companion to the String Quartet*. Cambridge: Cambridge University Press, 185–209.

Swinney, D. (1979) Lexical access during sentence comprehension: (Re)consideration of context effects. *Journal of Verbal Learning and Verbal Behaviour*, 18, 645–659.

Tagg, P. (2000) *Kojak: 50 Seconds of Television Music*. New York: The Mass Media Music Scholars' Press, Inc.

Tagg, P., and Clarida, B. (2003) *Ten Little Title Tunes*. New York: The Mass Media Music Scholars' Press, Inc.

Tarasti, E. (1994) *A Theory of Musical Semiotics*. Bloomington : Indiana University Press.

Temperley, D. (2001) *The Cognition of Basic Musical Structures*. Cambridge MA: MIT Press.

Todd, N. P. (1992) The dynamics of dynamics: a model of musical expression. *Journal of the Acoustical Society of America*, 91, 3540–3550.

———. (1995) The kinematics of musical expression. *Journal of the Acoustical Society of America*, 97, 1940–1949.

———. (1999) Motion in music: a neurobiological perspective. *Music Perception*, 17, 115–126.

Todd, P. M., and Loy, D. G., eds. (1991) *Music and Connectionism*. Cambridge, MA: MIT Press.

Toop, D. (1995) *Ocean of Sound. Aether Talk, Ambient Sound and Imaginary Worlds*. London: Serpent's Tail.

Truax, B. (1984) *Acoustic Communication*. Norwood, NJ: Ablex Publishing.

Truslit, A. (1938) *Gestaltung und Bewegung in der Musik*. Berlin: Chr. Friedrich Vieweg.

Vanderveer, N. J. (1979) Ecological Acoustics. Human Perception of Environmental Sounds. Doctoral Thesis, Dissertation Abstracts International, 40/09B, 4543 (University Microfilms No. 8004002).

Warren, W., and Verbrugge, R. (1984) Auditory perception of breaking and bouncing events: a case study in ecological acoustics. *Journal of Experimental Psychology: Human Perception and Performance*, 10, 704–712.

Watt, R. J., and Ash, R. L. (1998) A psychological investigation of meaning in music. *Musicae Scientiae*, 2, 33–54.

Whittall, A. (1999) Autonomy/heteronomy: The contexts of musicology. In N. Cook and M. Everist, eds., *Rethinking Music*. Oxford: Oxford University Press, 73–101.

Windsor, W. L. (1994) Using auditory information for events in electroacoustic music. *Contemporary Music Review*, 10, 85–93.

———. (1995) A Perceptual Approach to the Description and Analysis of Acousmatic Music. Unpublished PhD thesis, City University, London.

———. (1996a) Perception and Signification in Electroacoustic Music. In R. Monelle and C. T. Gray, eds., *Song and Signification*. Edinburgh University Faculty of Music.

———. (1996b) Autonomy, mimesis and mechanical reproduction in contemporary music. *Contemporary Music Review*, 15, 139–150.

———. (1997) Frequency structure in electroacoustic music: ideology, function and perception. *Organised Sound*, 2, 77–82.

———. (2000) Through and around the acousmatic: the interpretation of electroacoustic sounds. In S. Emmerson, ed., *Music, Electronic Media and Culture*. Aldershot: Ashgate Press, 7–33.

————. (2002) The affordances of music. Paper presented at the 7th European Workshop on Ecological Psychology. Bendor, France; 4–6 July 2002.

————. (2004) An ecological approach to semiotics. *Journal of the Theory of Social Behaviour*, 34, 179–198.

Yeston, M. (1976) *The Stratification of Musical Rhythm*. New Haven: Yale University Press.

Young, J. (1996) Imagining the source: The interplay of realism and abstraction in electroacoustic music. *Contemporary Music Review*, 15, 73–93.

Zbikowski, L. M. (2002) *Conceptualizing Music. Cognitive Structure, Theory, and Analysis*. New York: Oxford University Press.

Index ～